Lauren Kay

101 INTRICATE PATTERN COLORING BOOK

THIS BOOK BELONGS TO

_ _ _ _ _ _ _

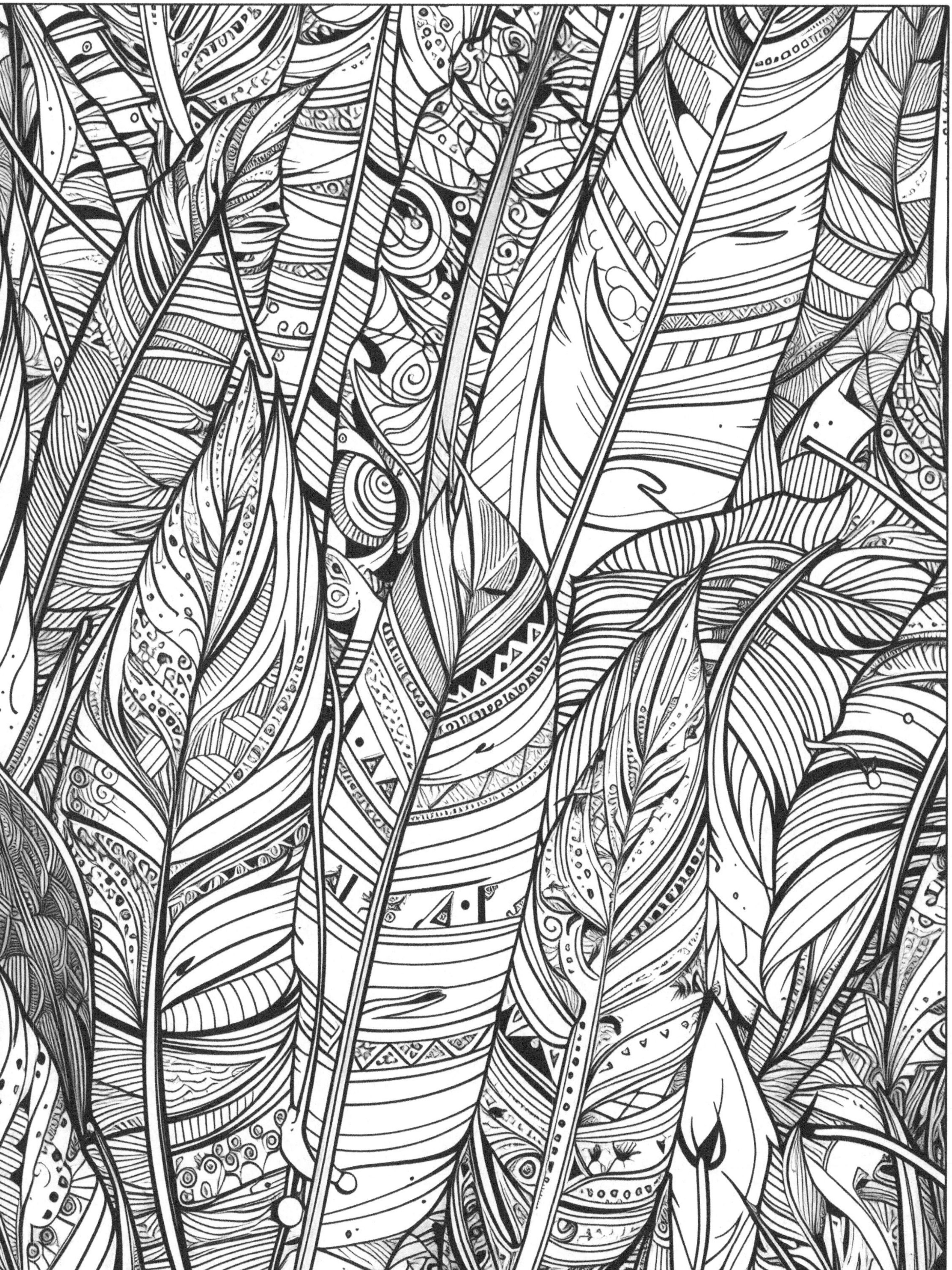

TEST COLOR PAGE

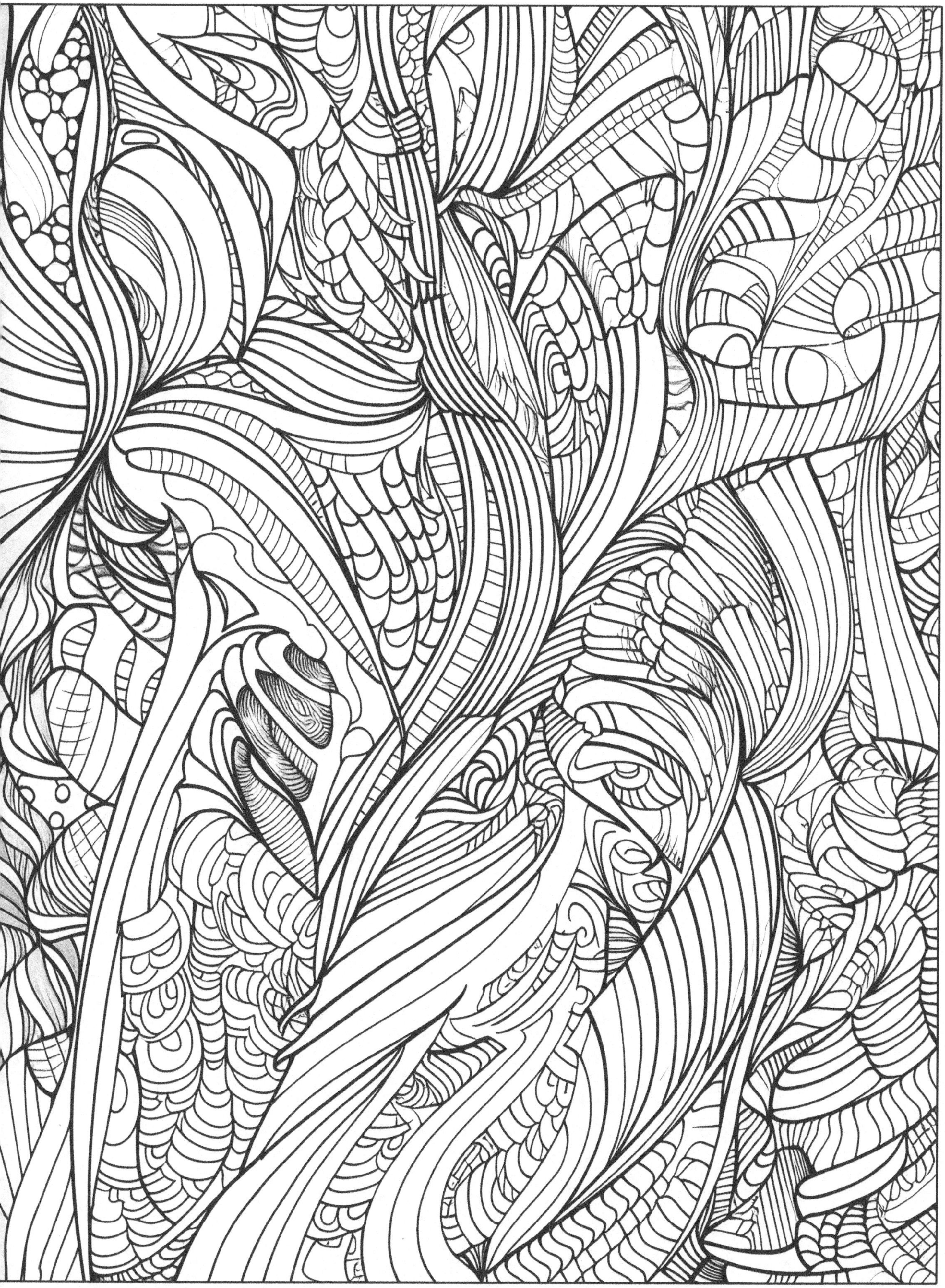

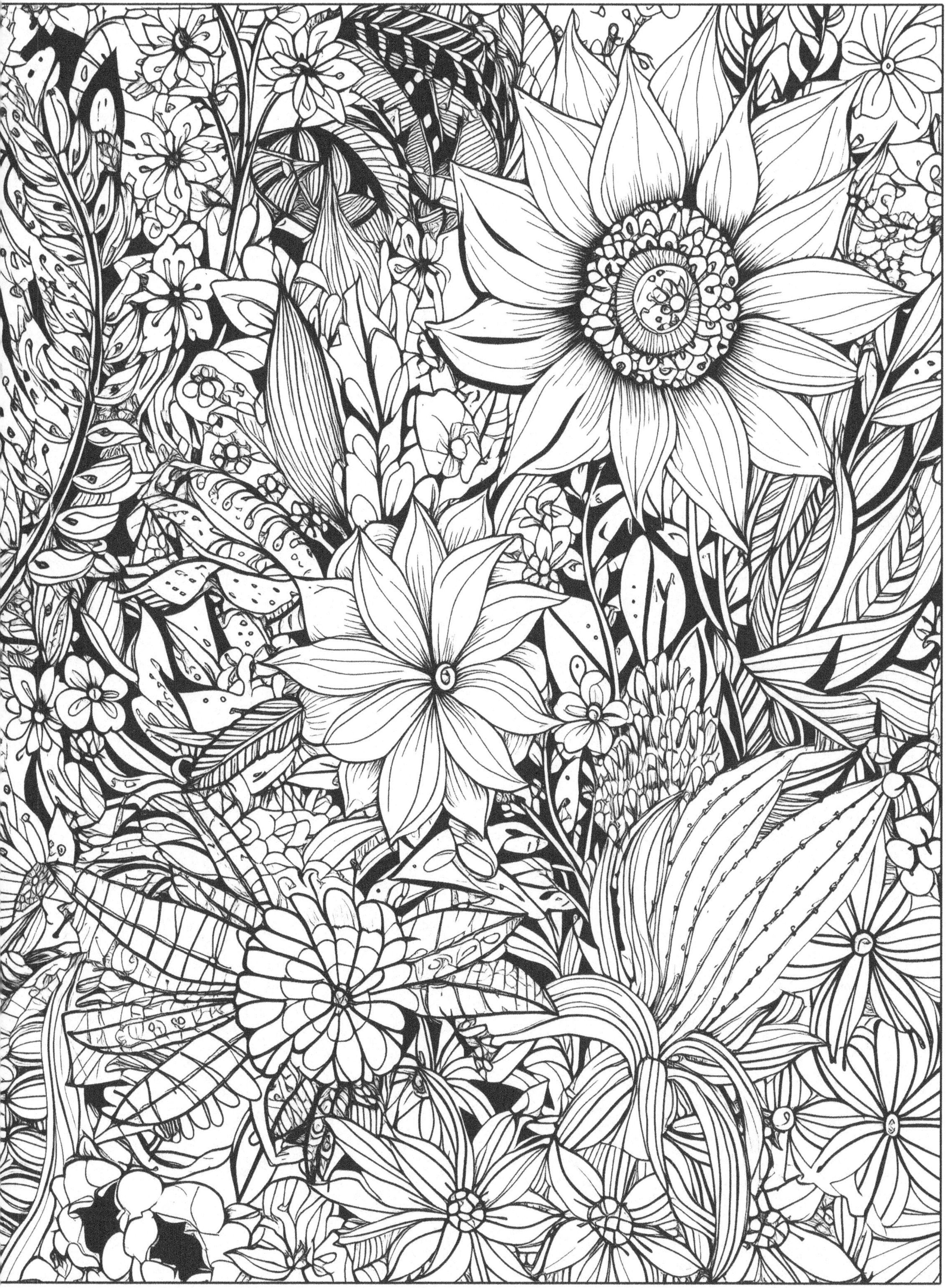

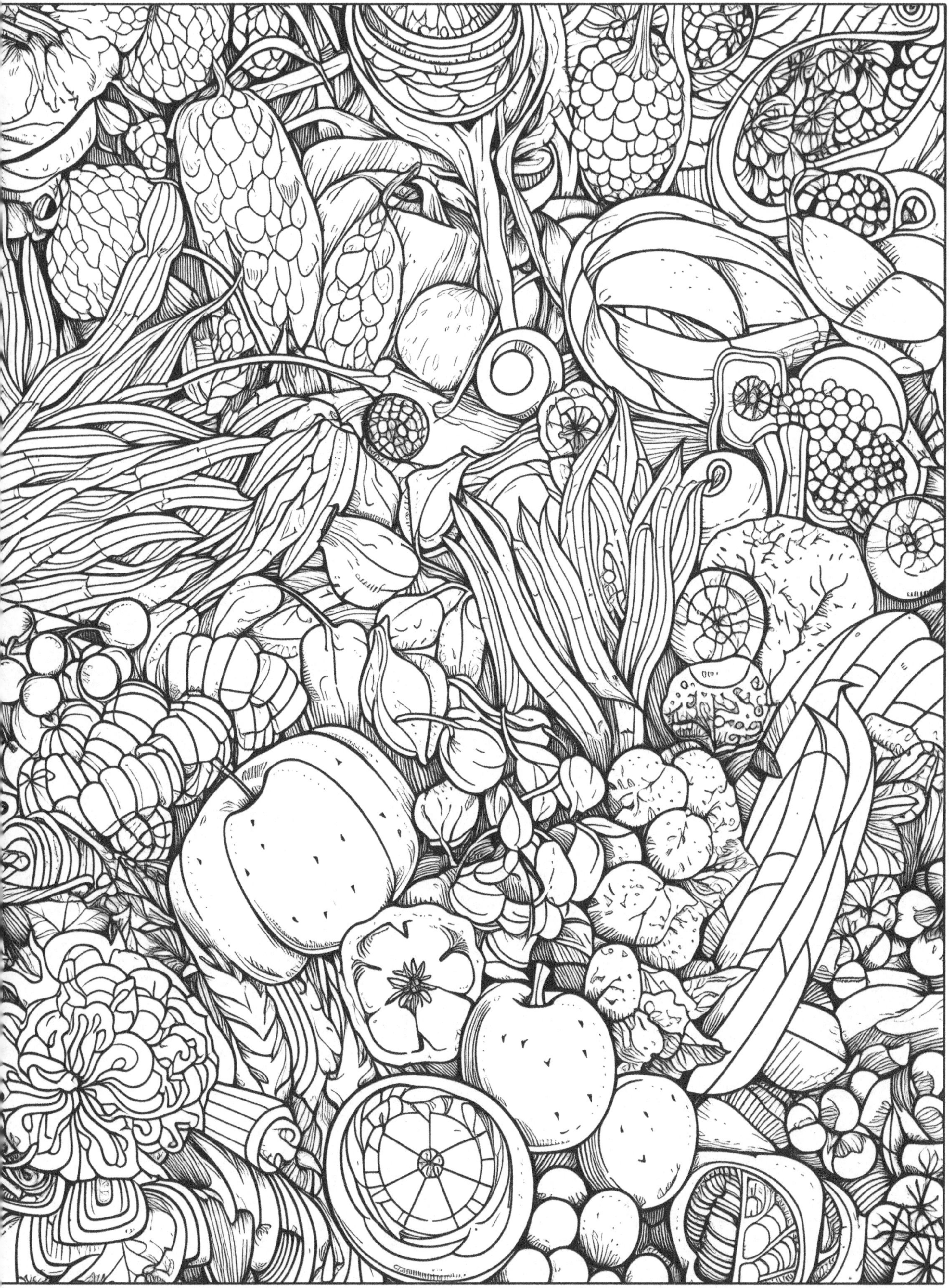

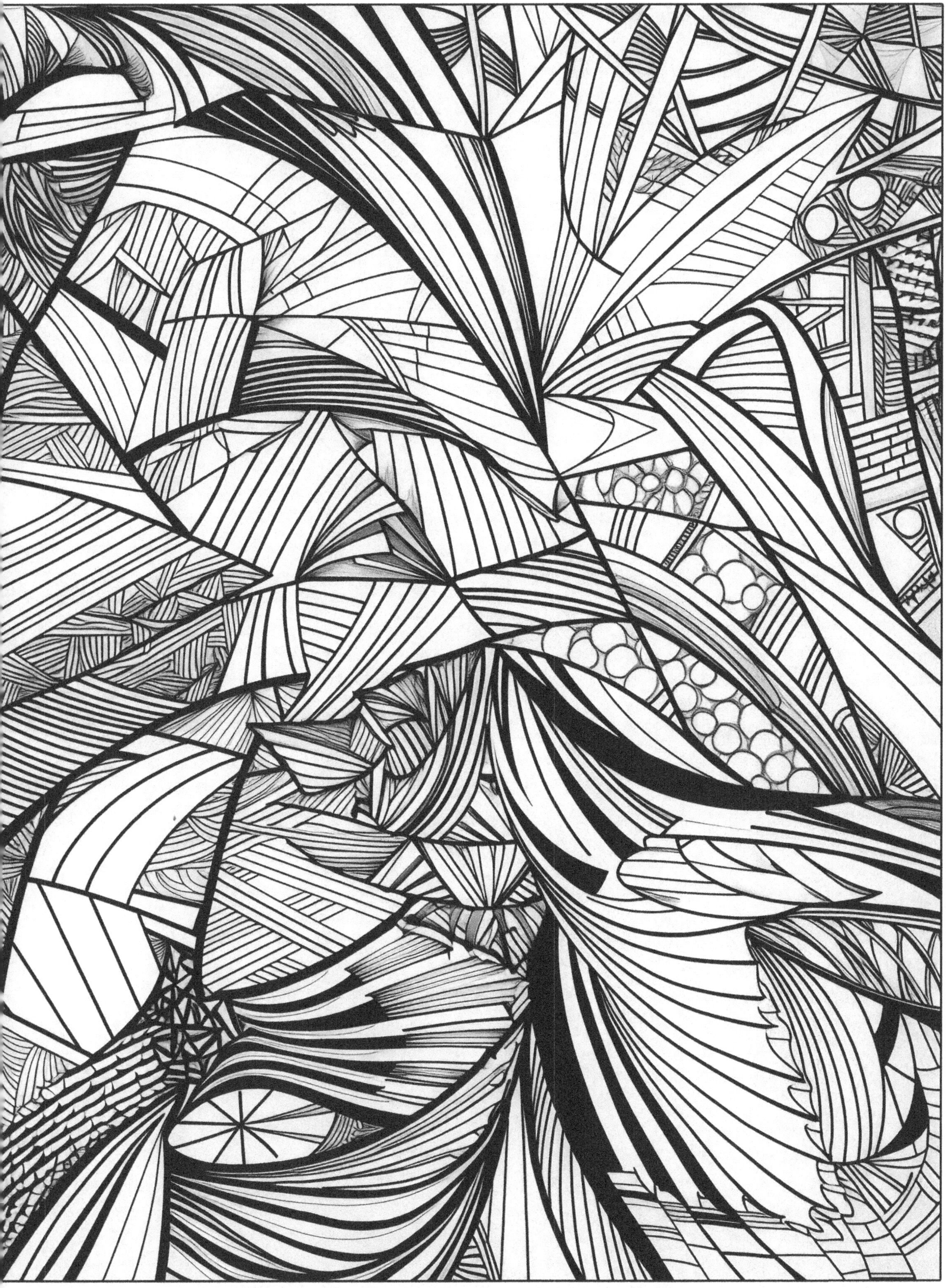

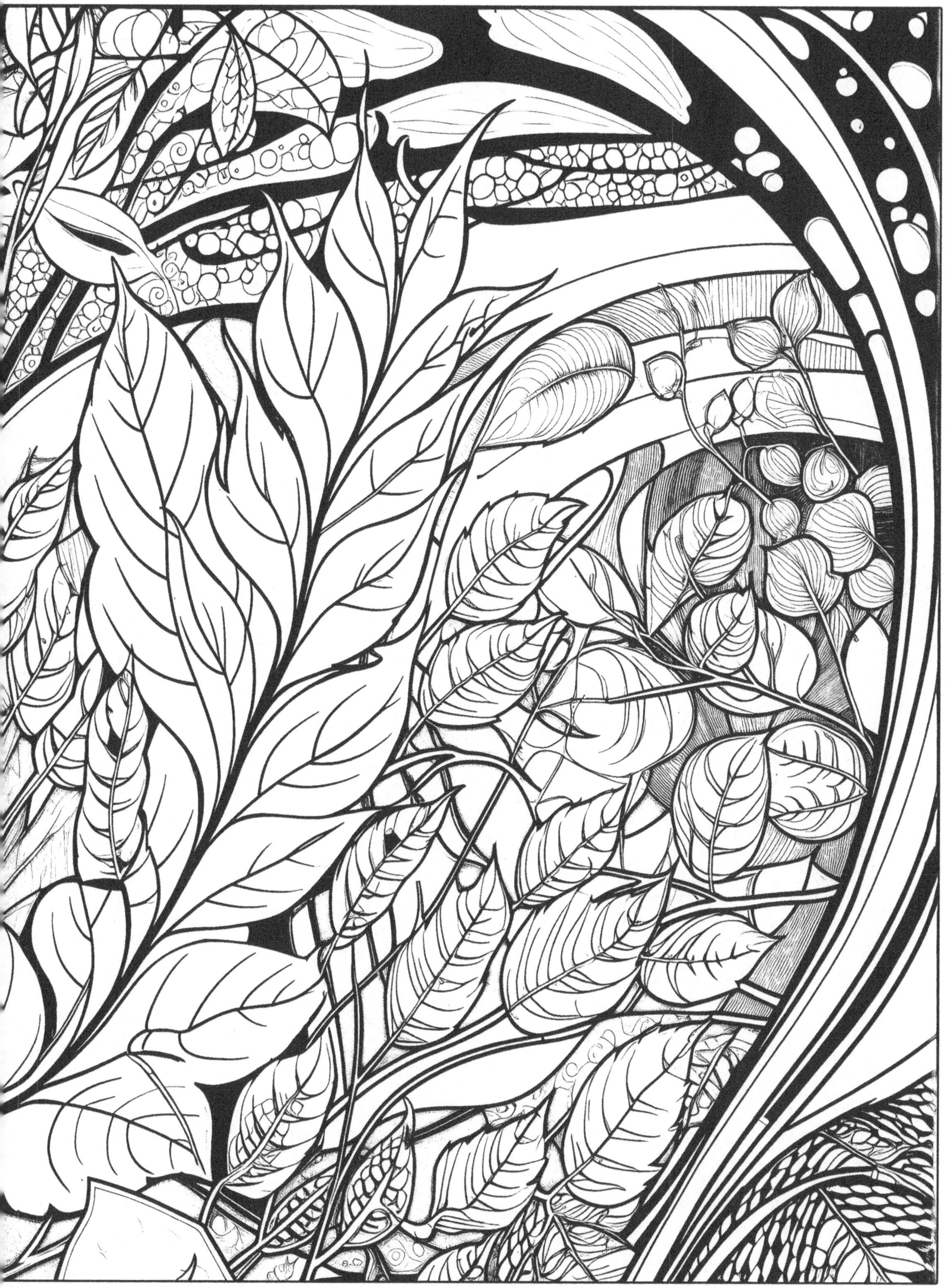

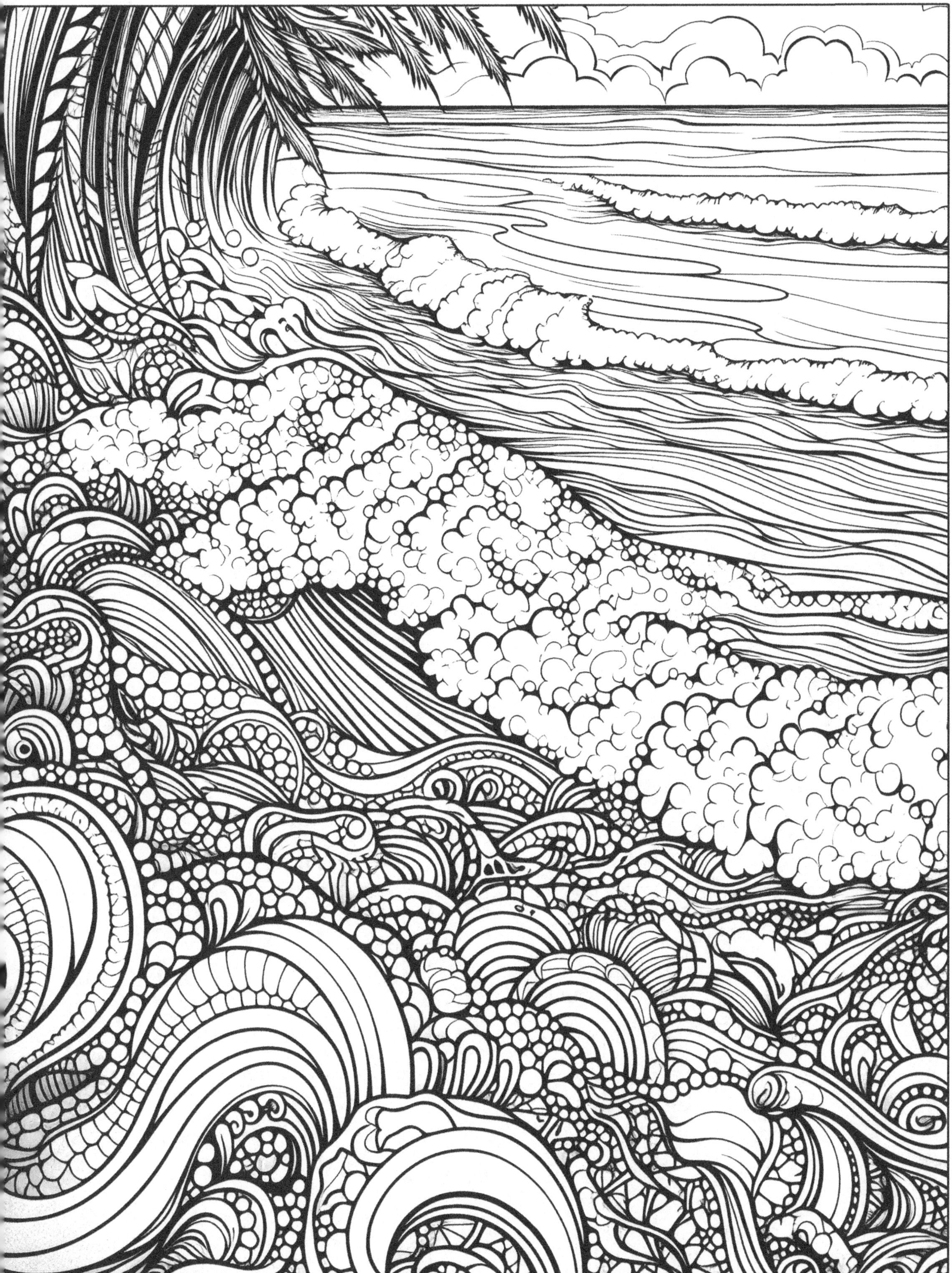

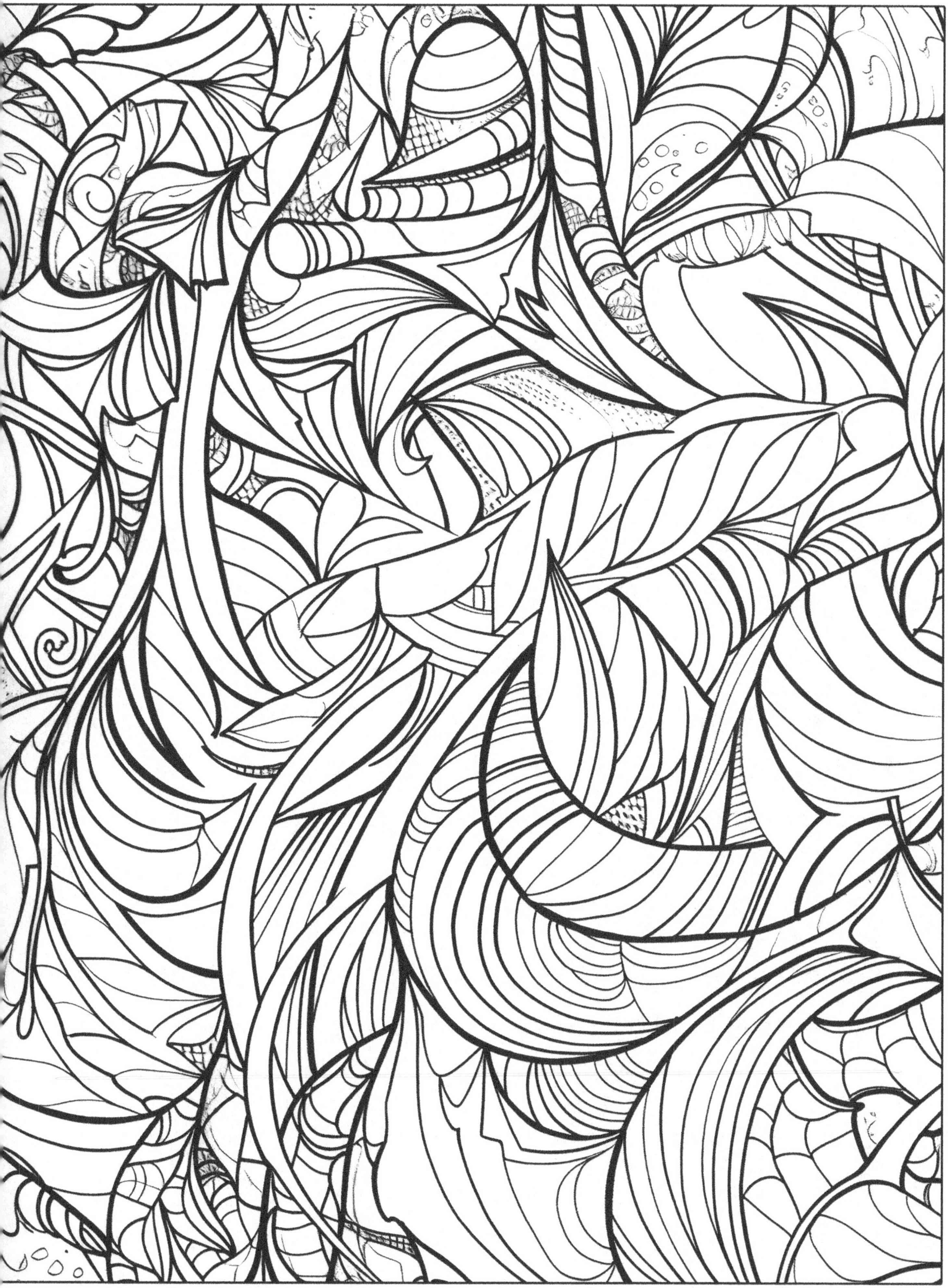

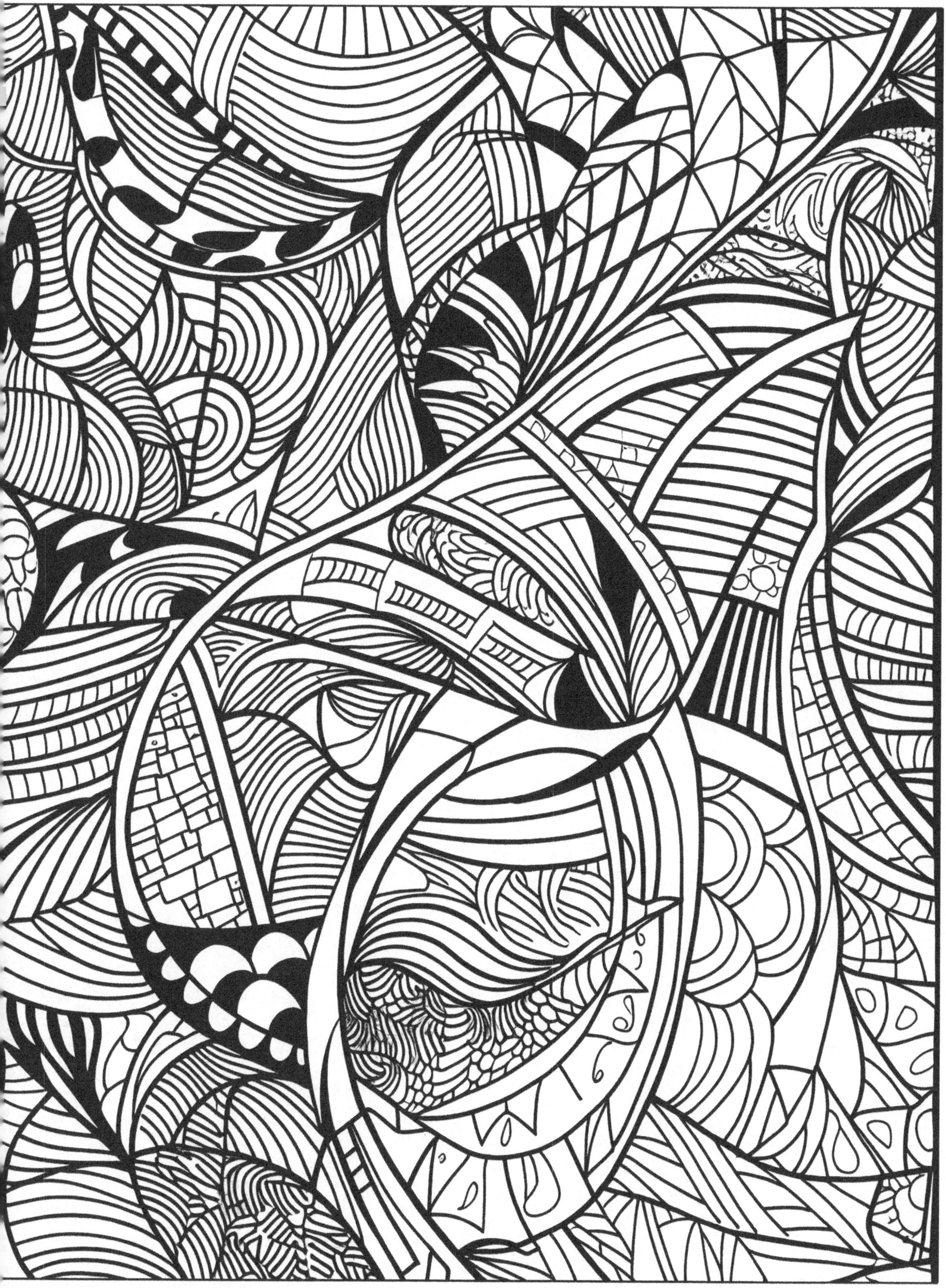

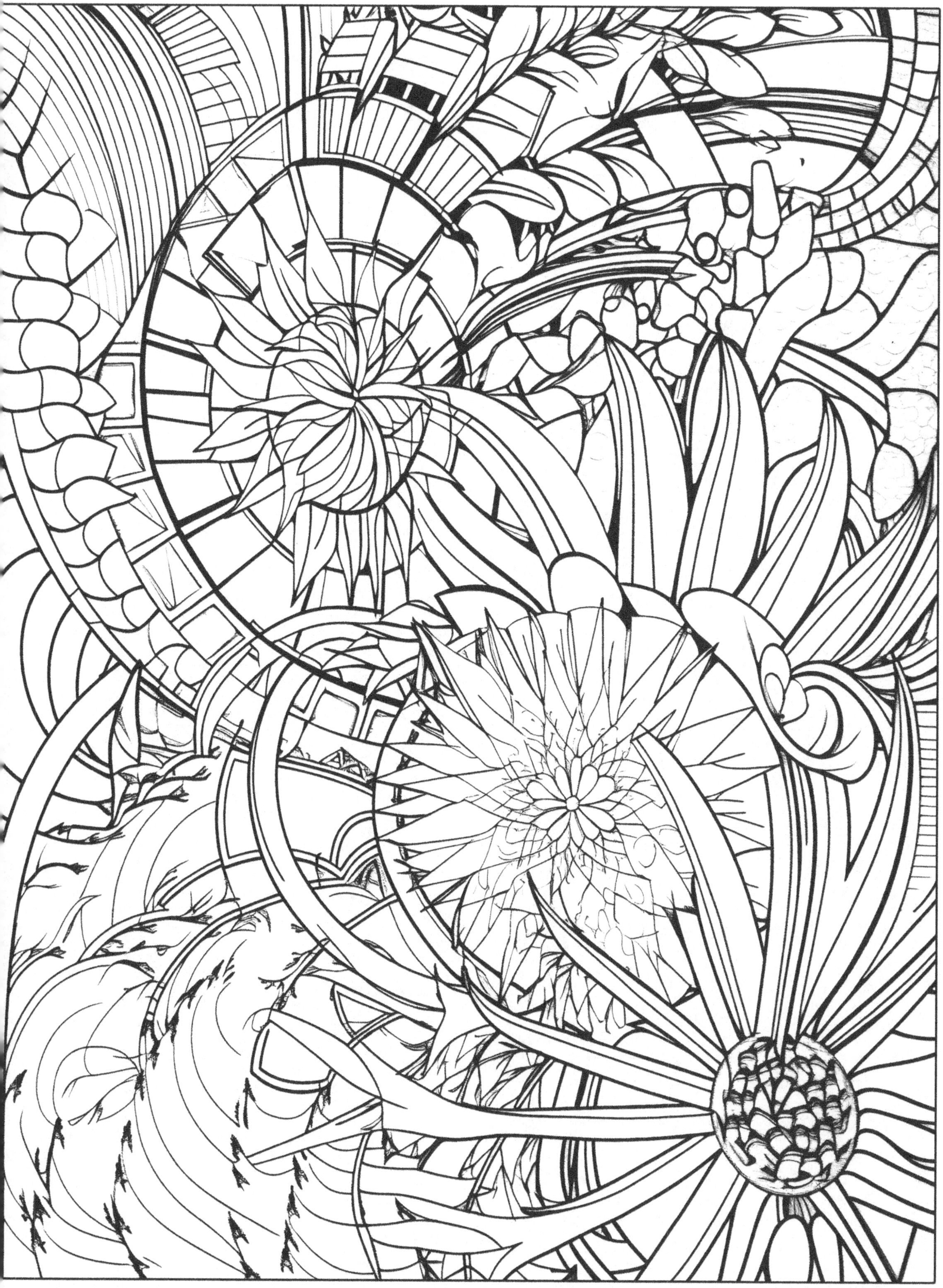

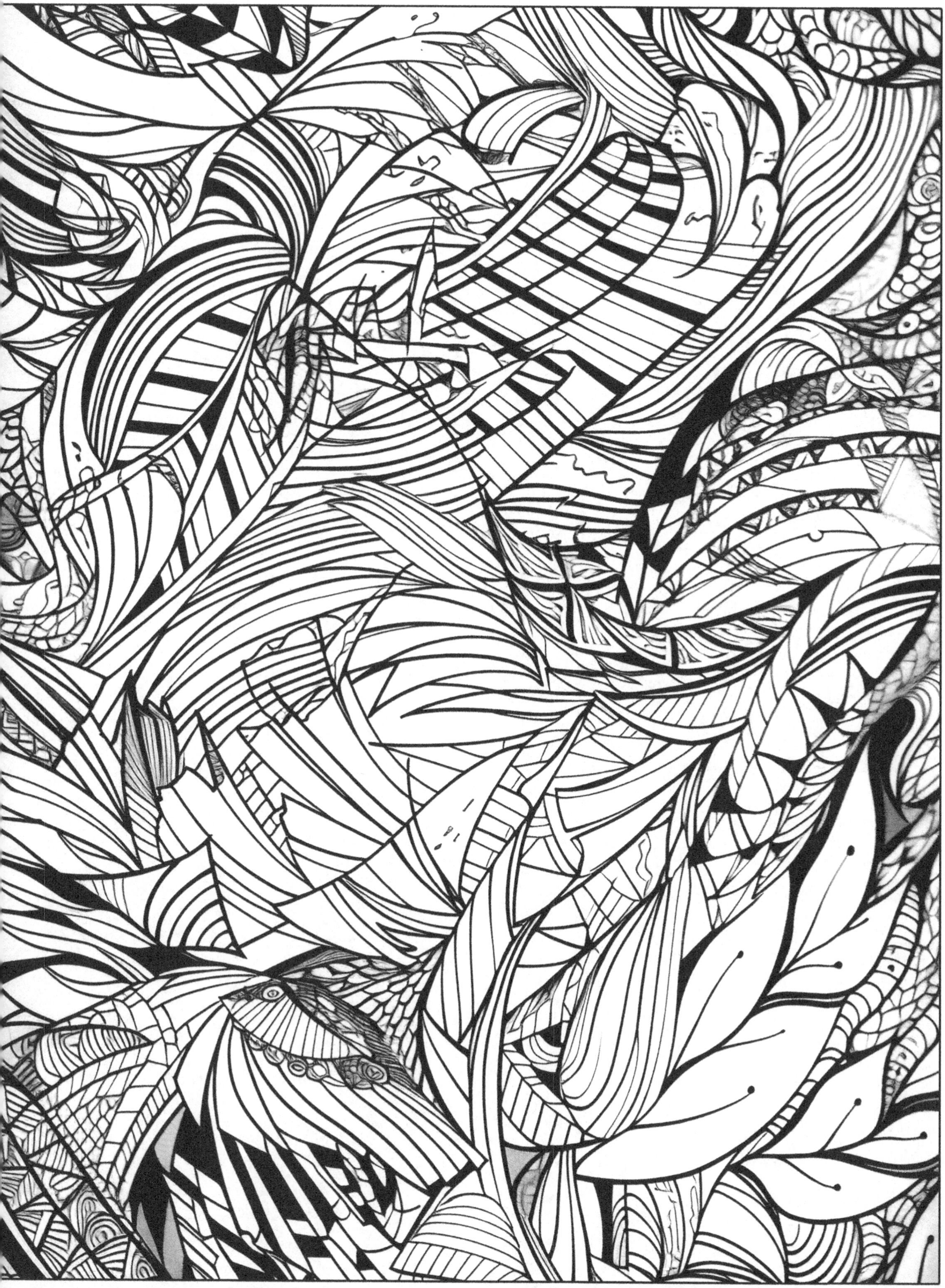

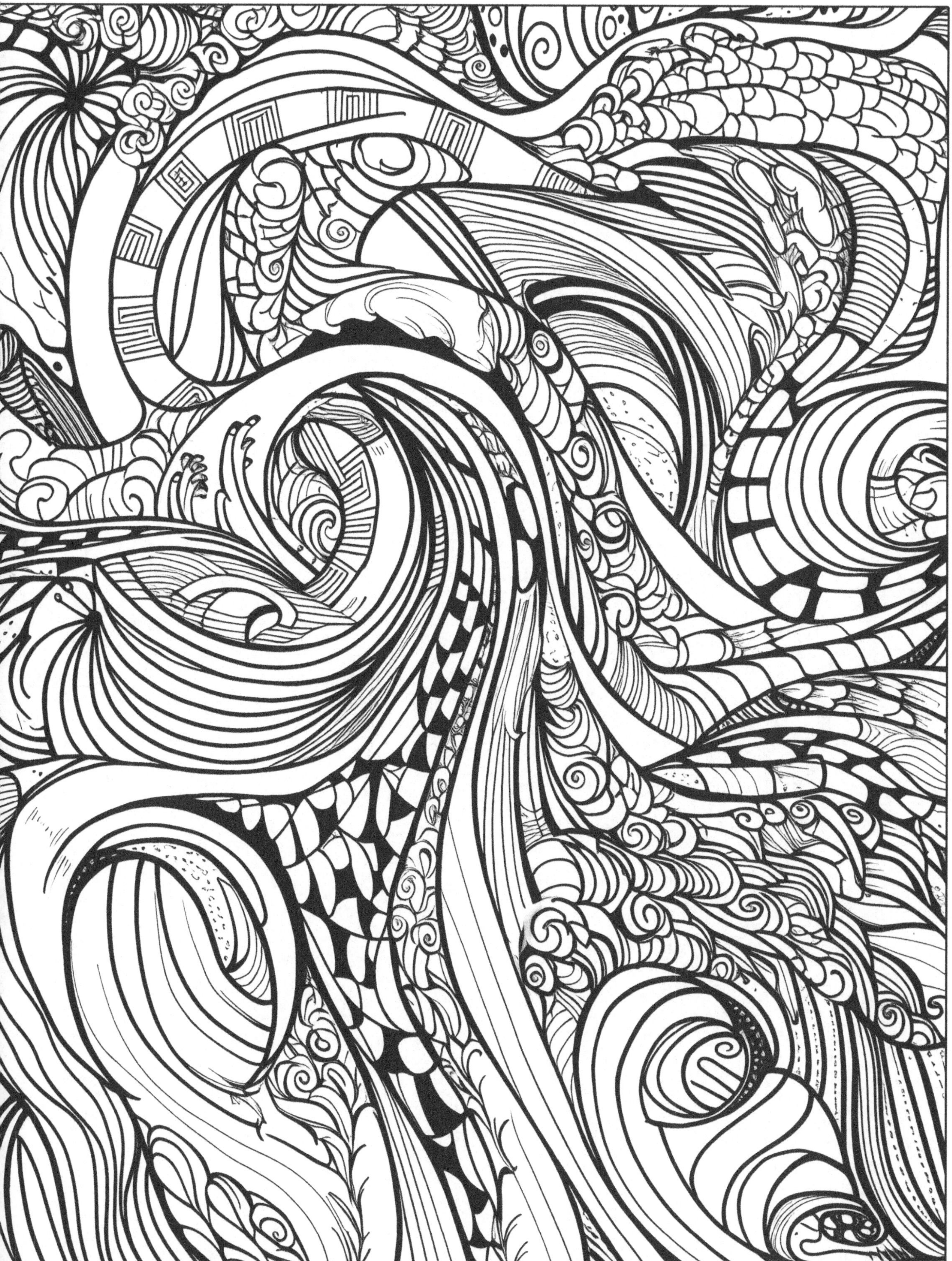

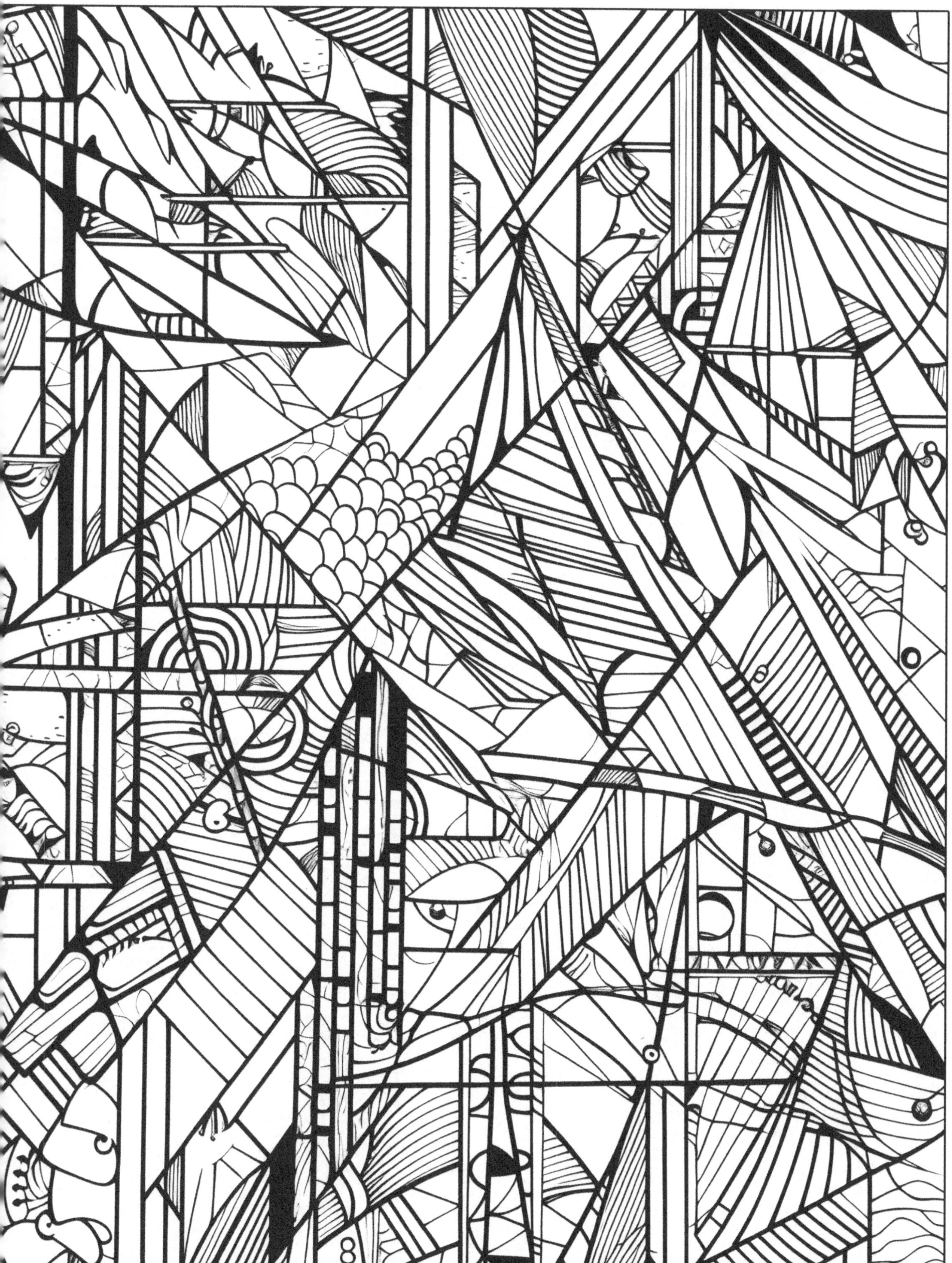

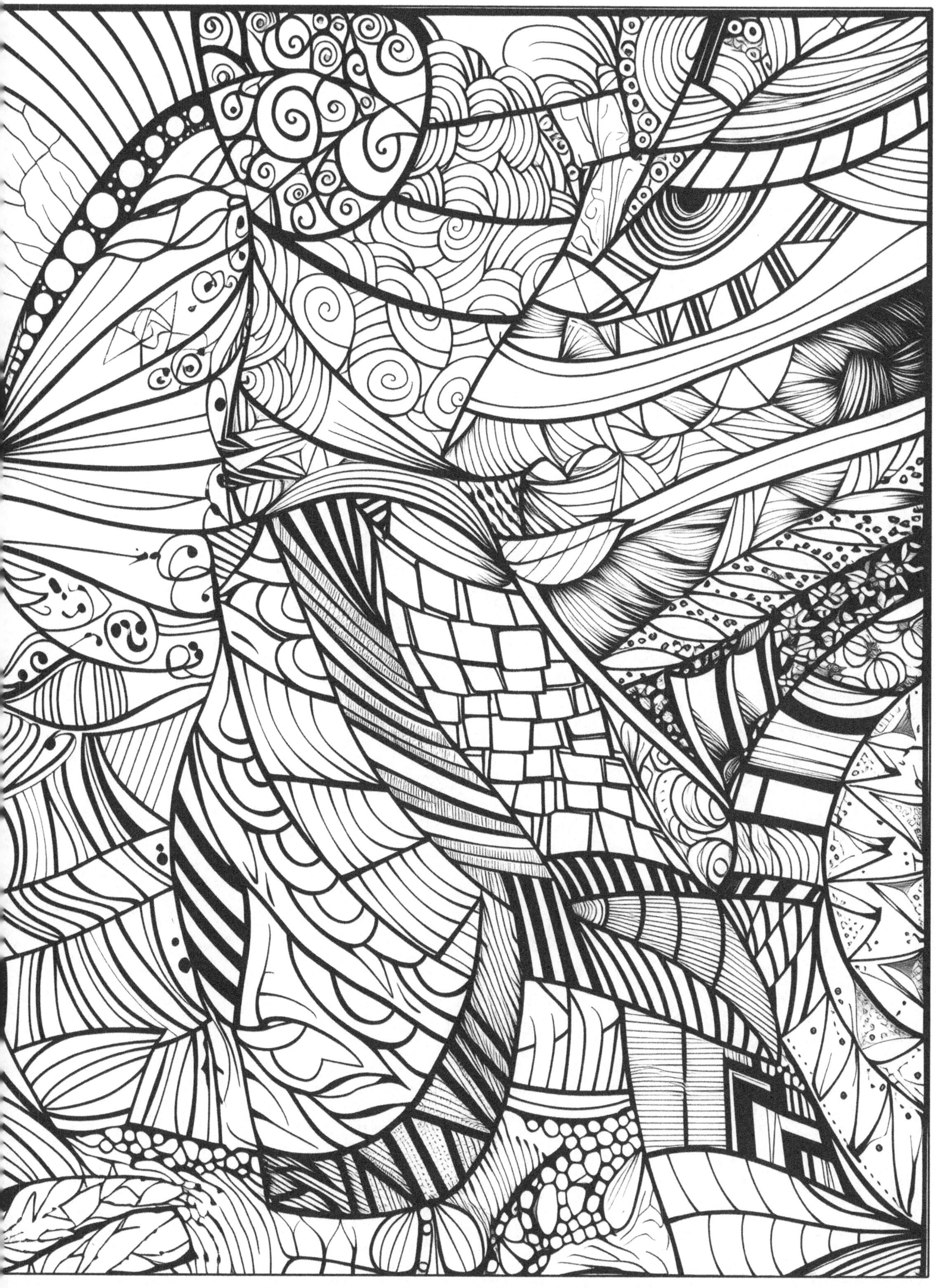

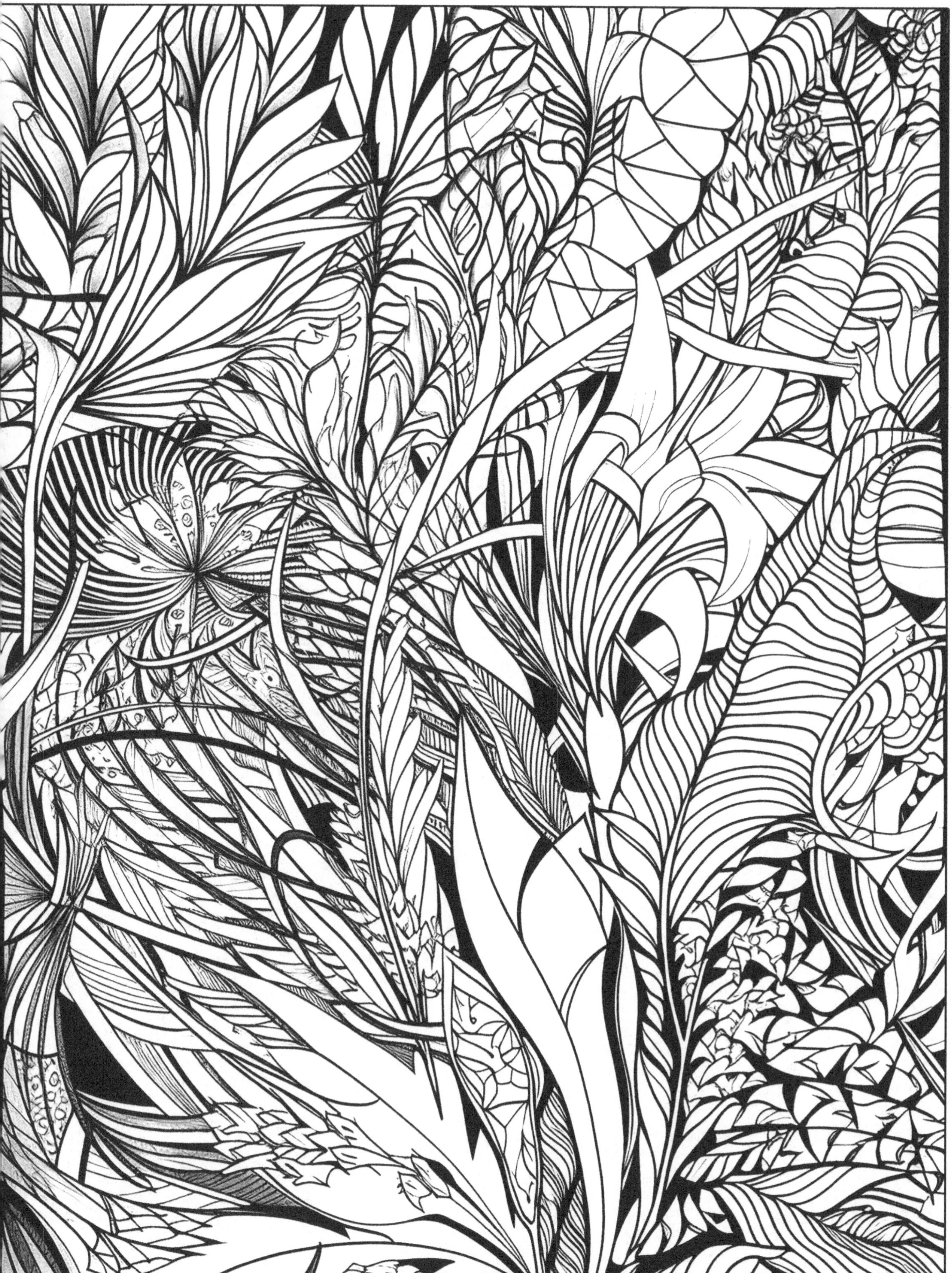

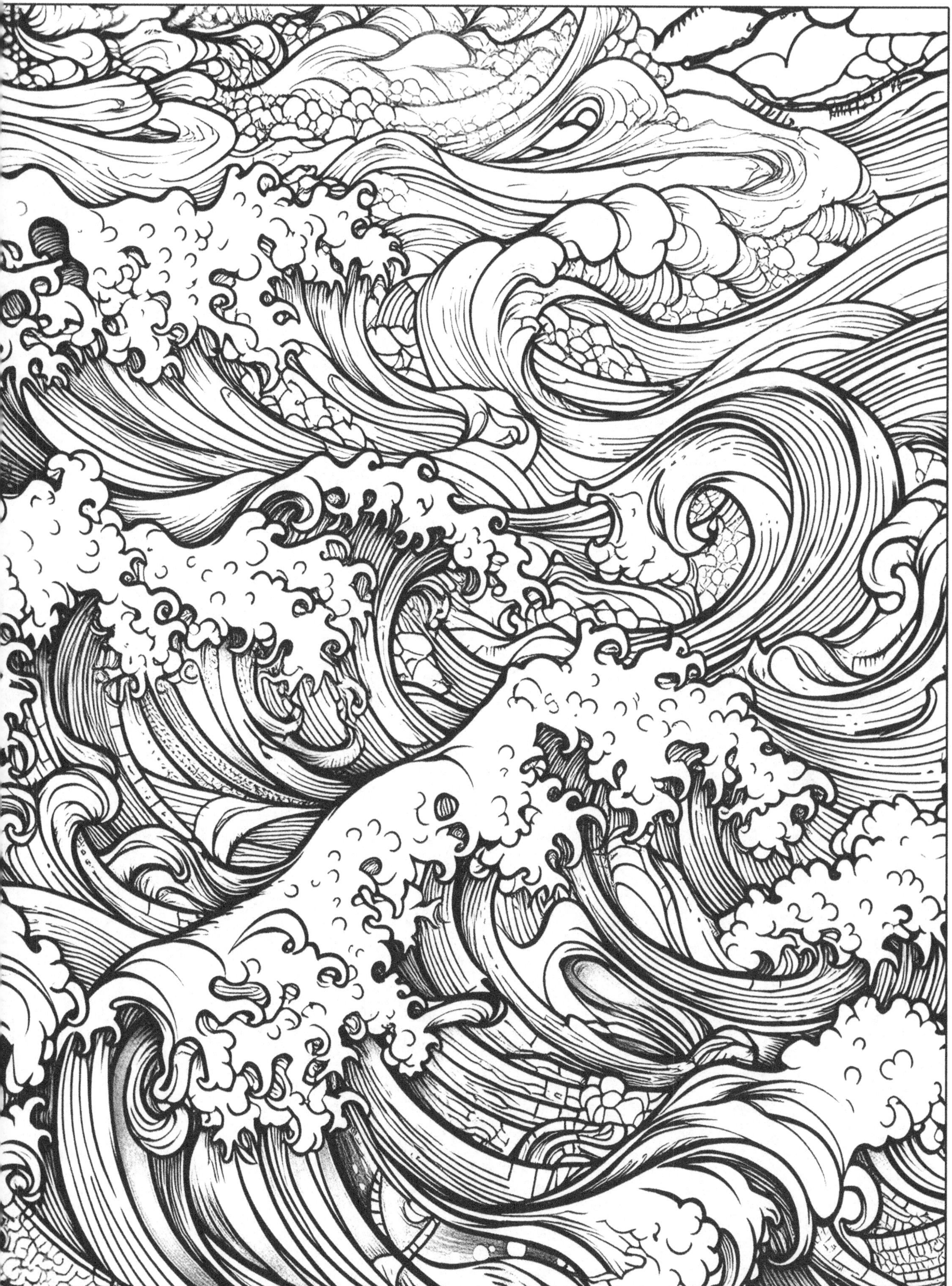

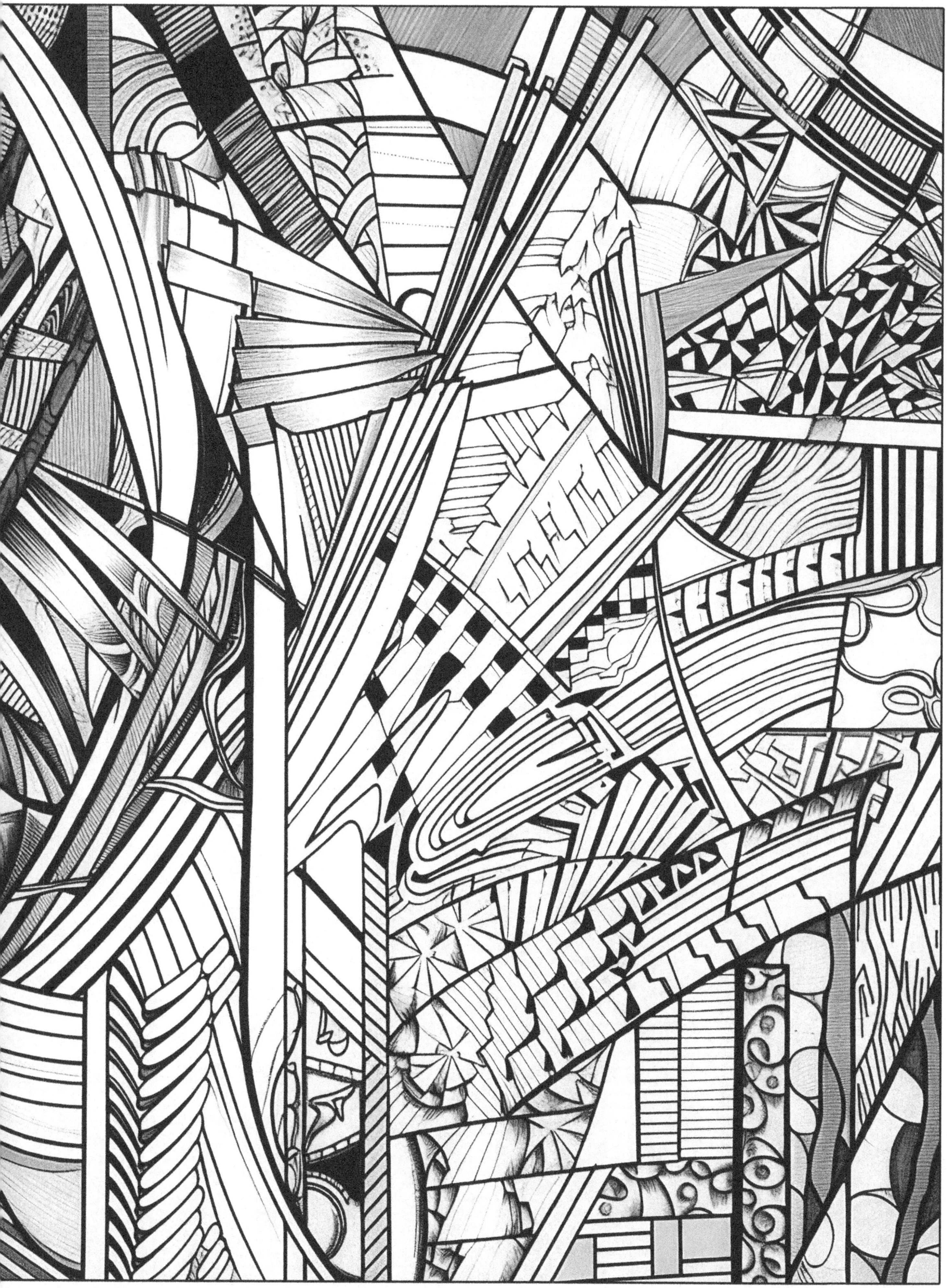

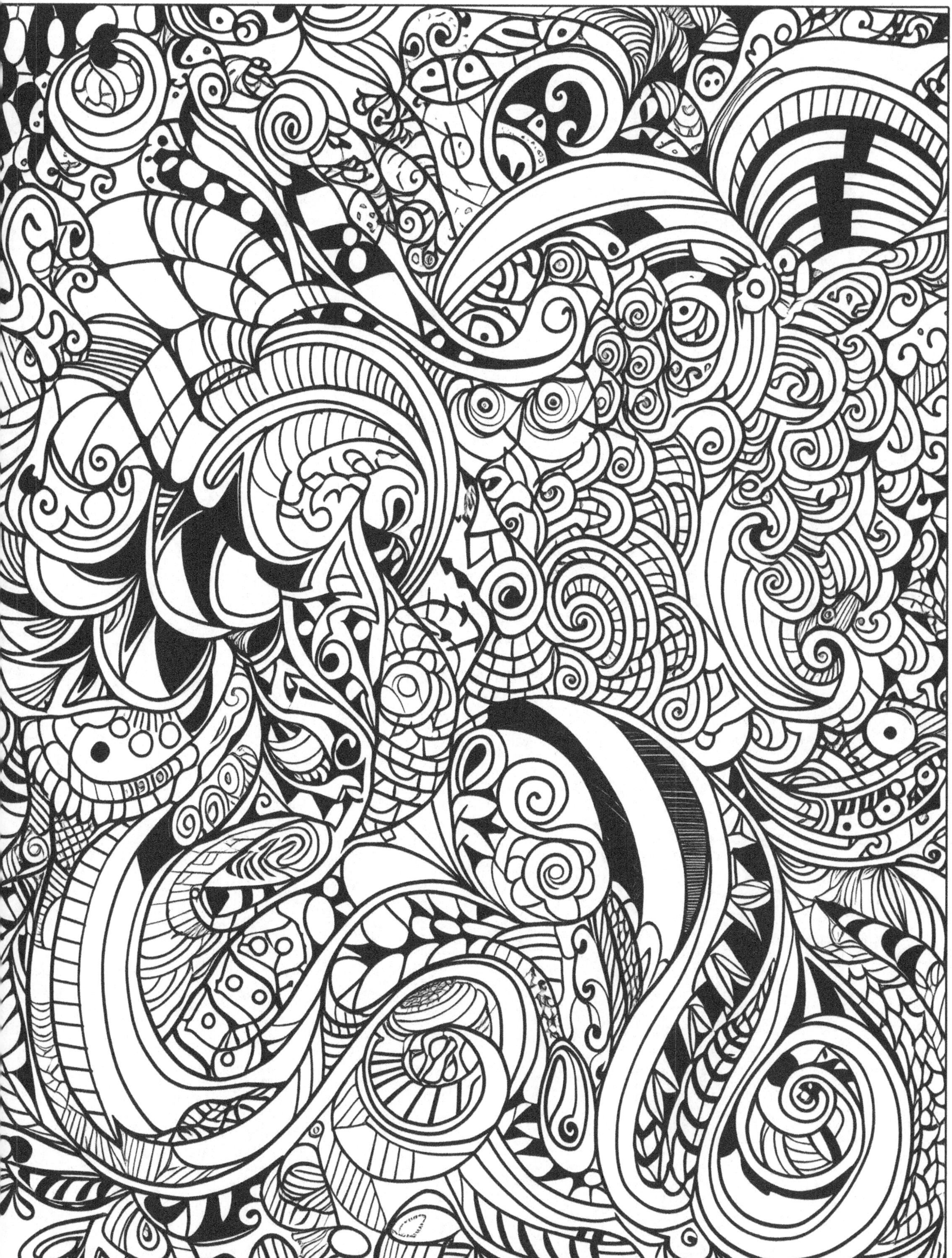

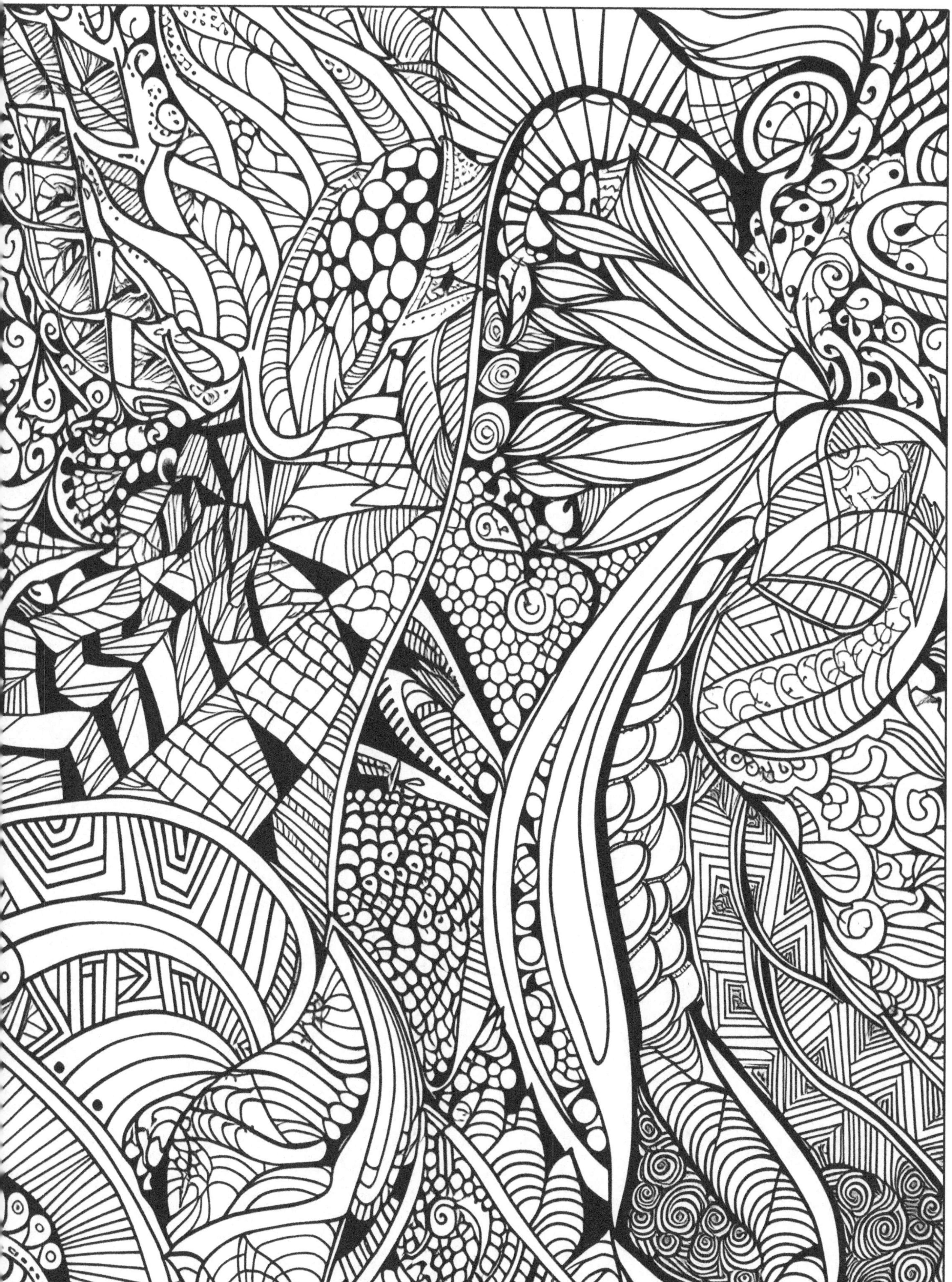

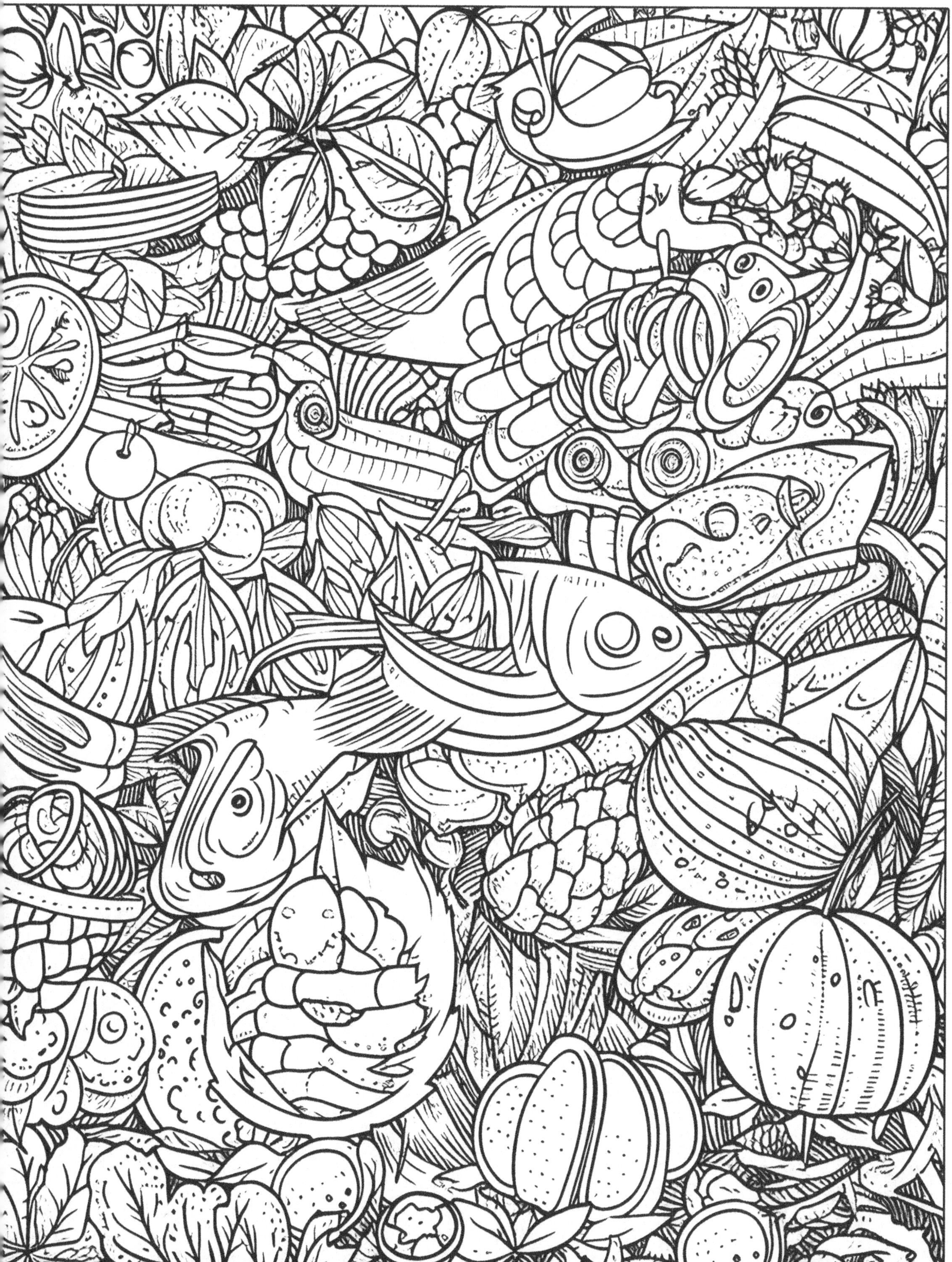

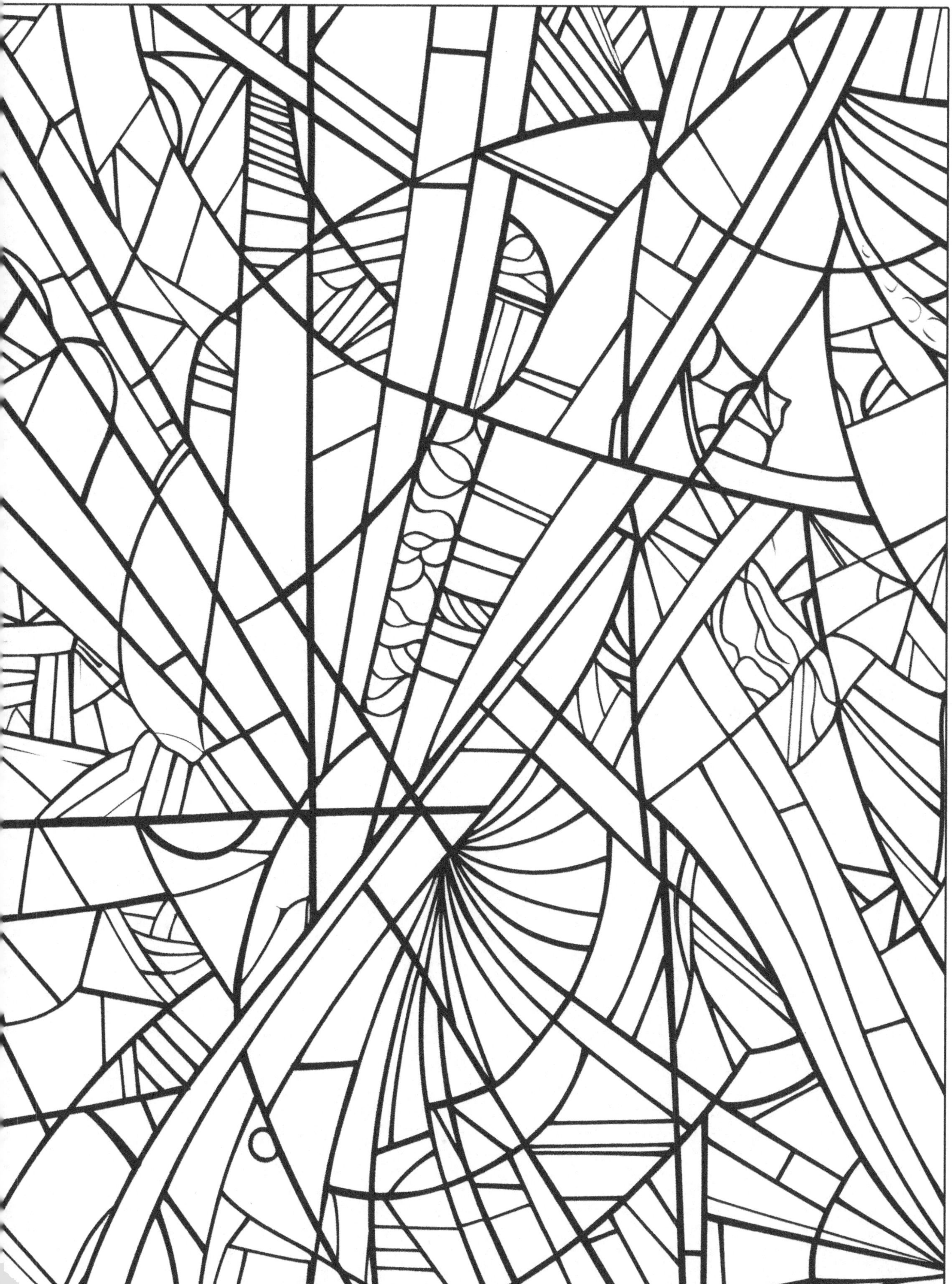

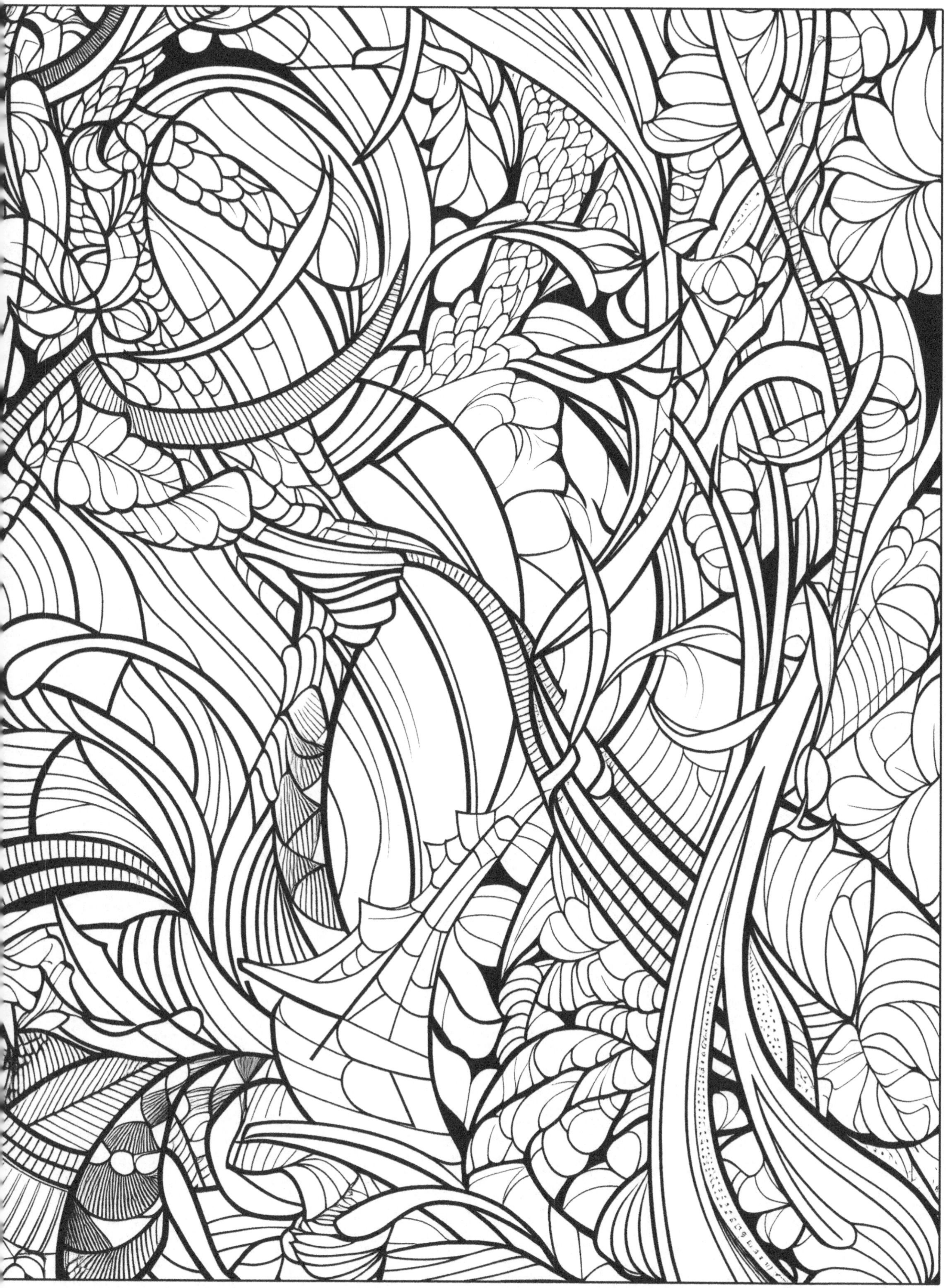

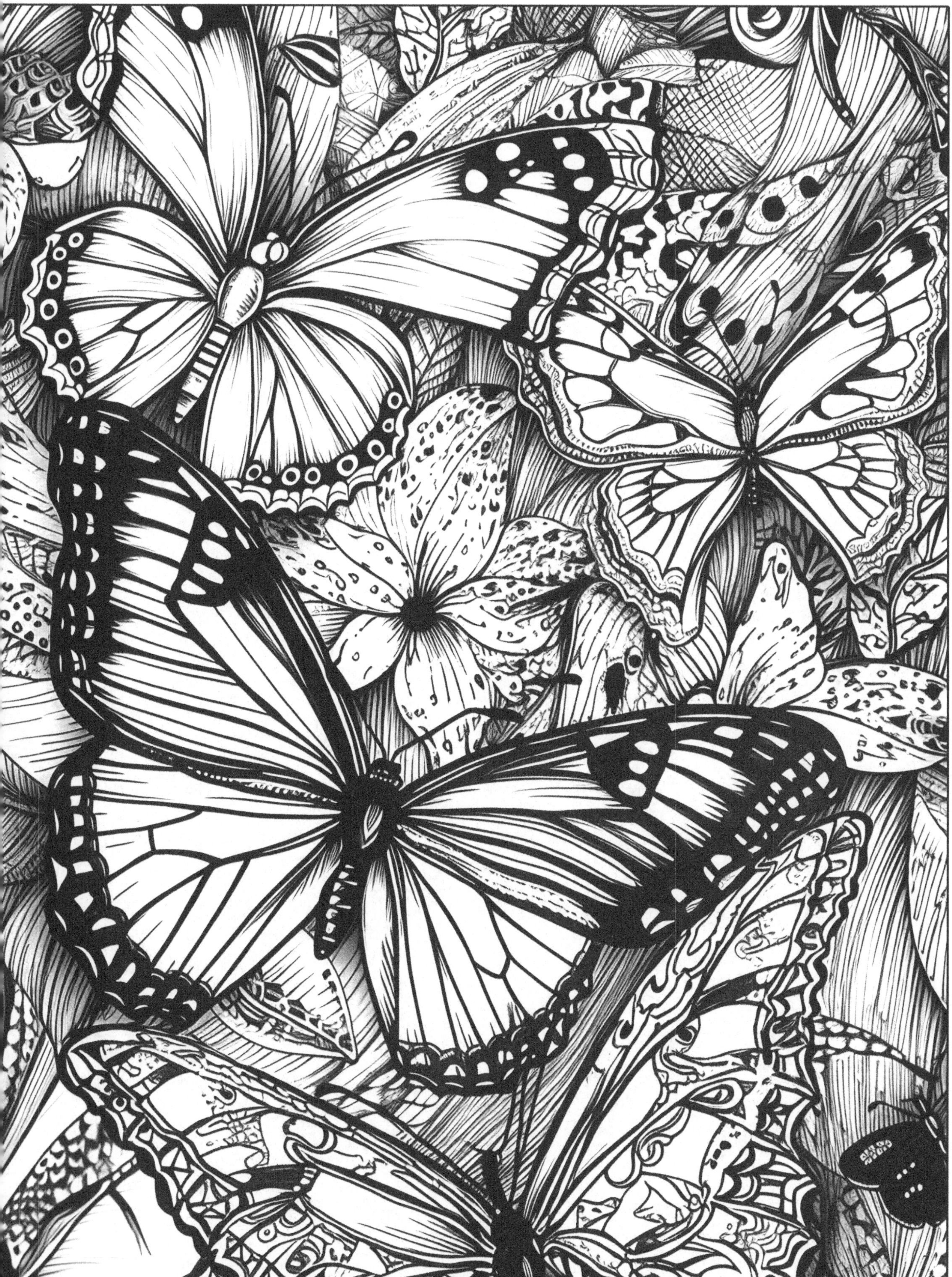

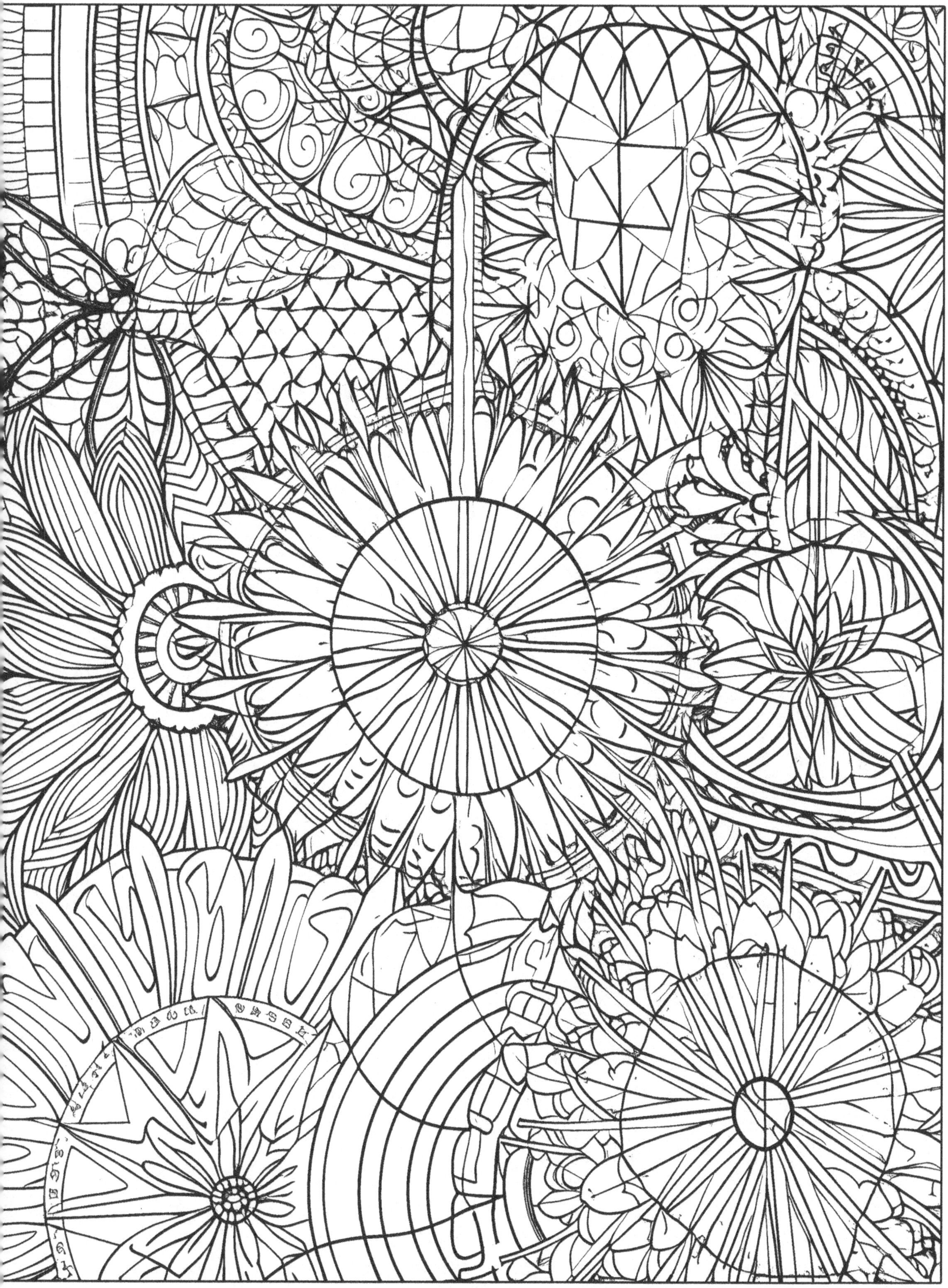

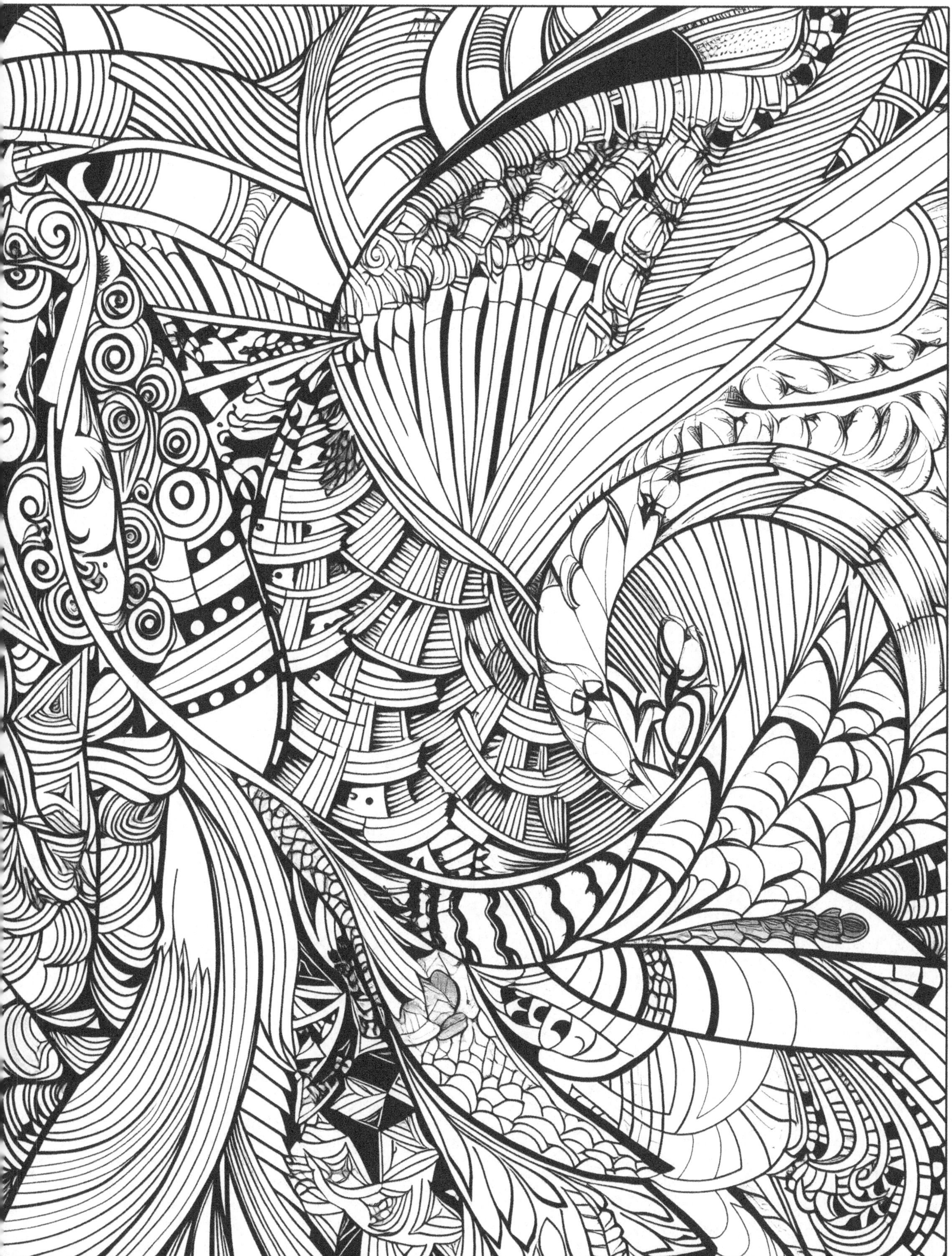

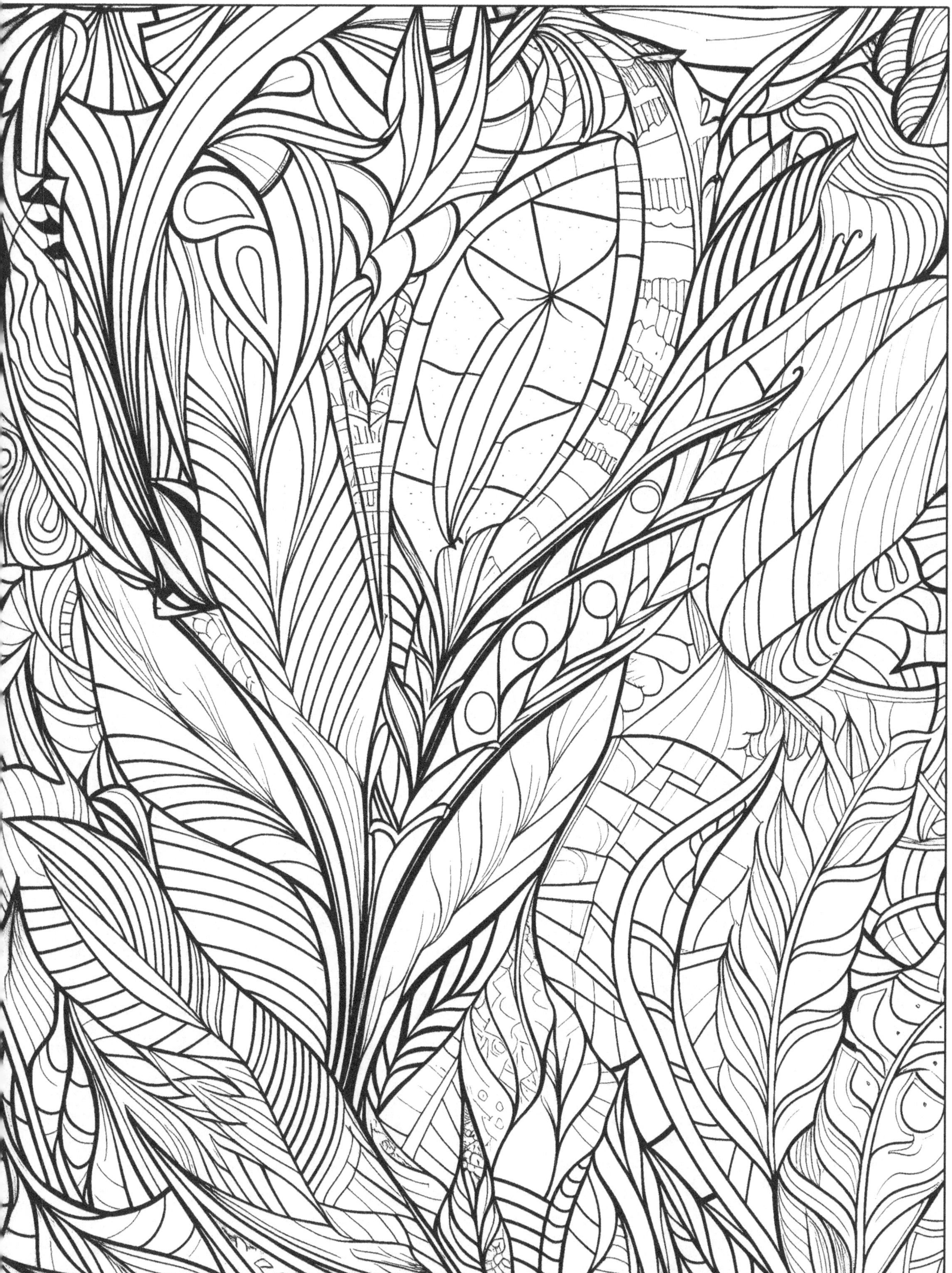

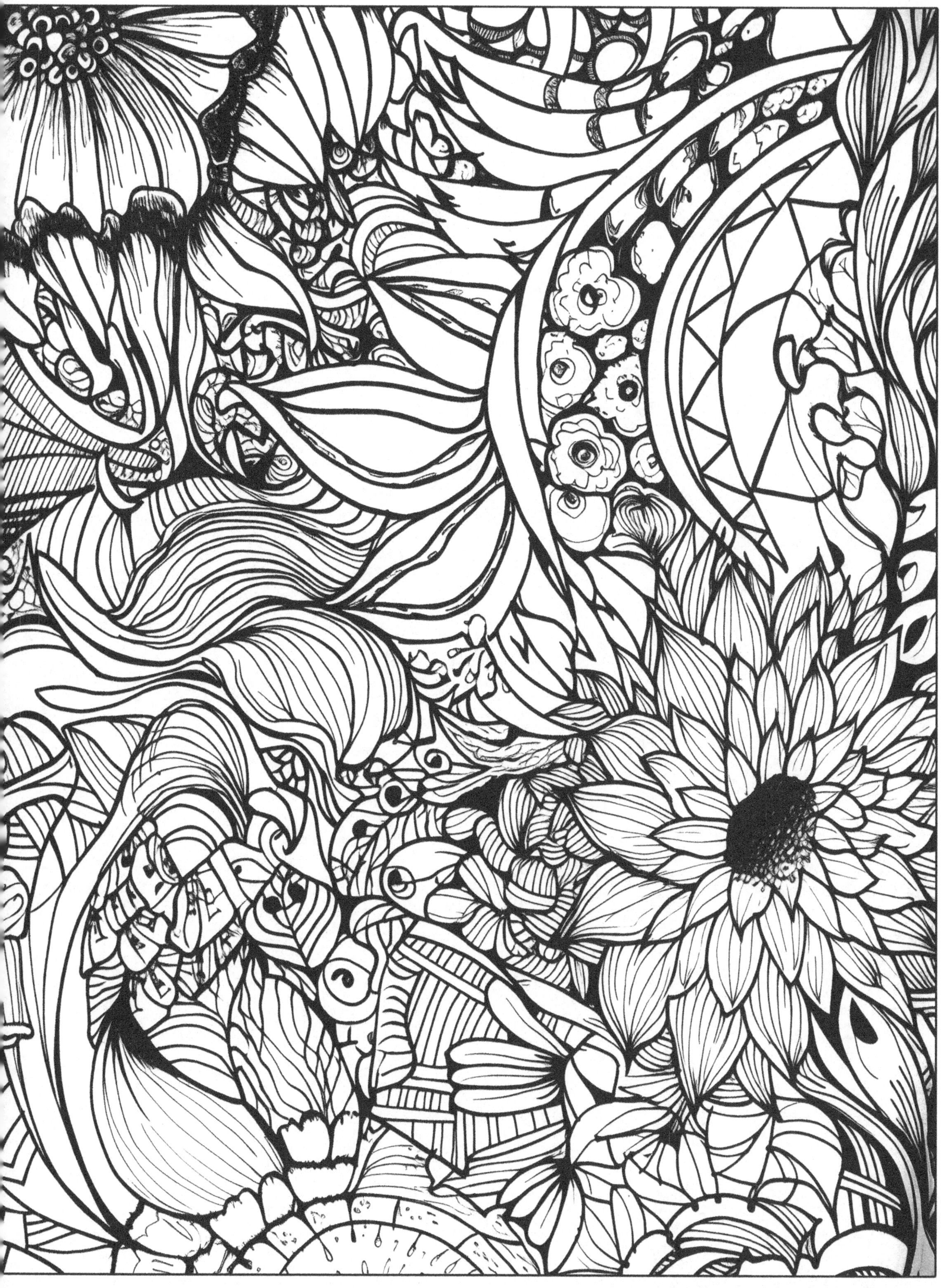

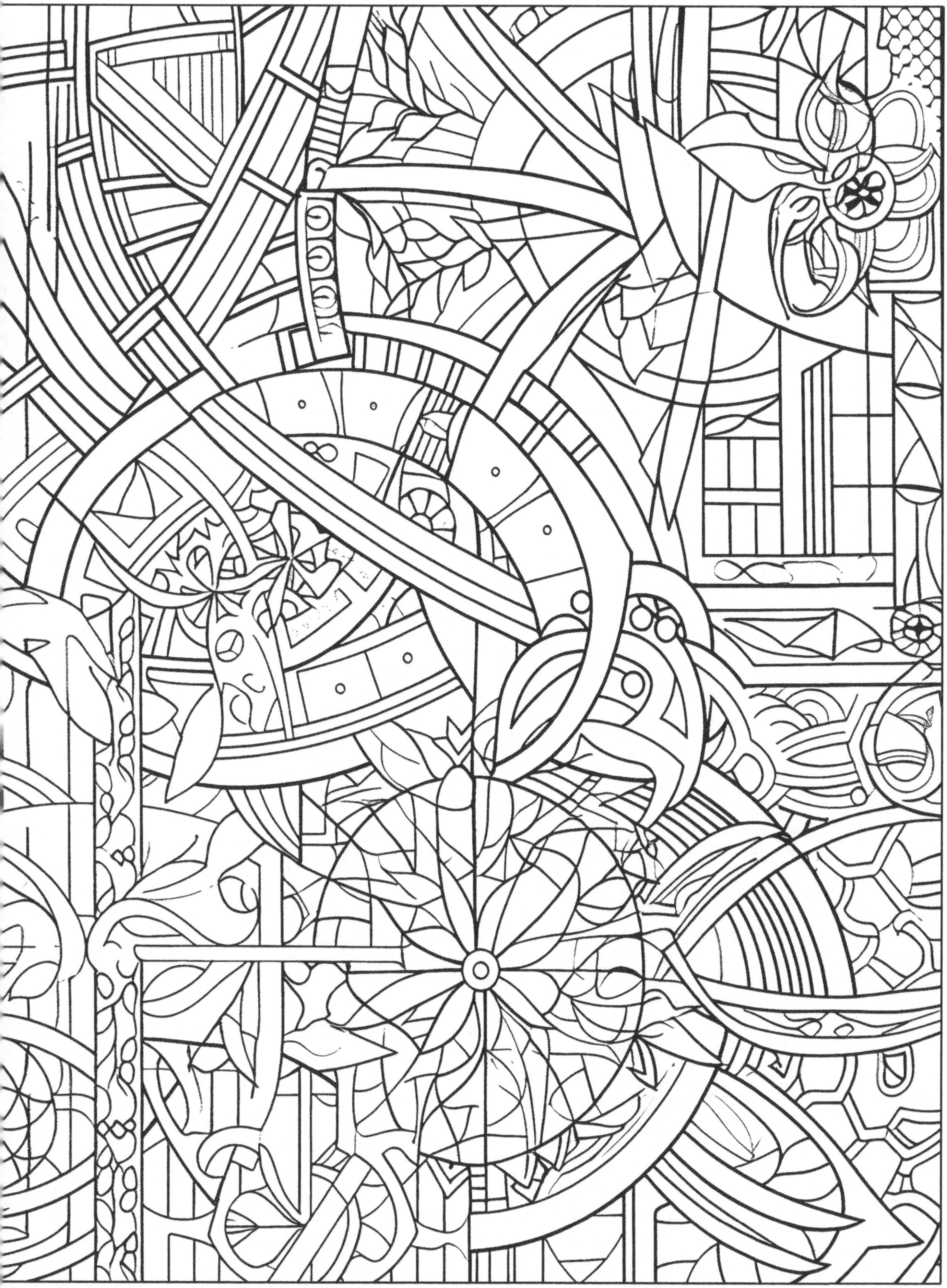

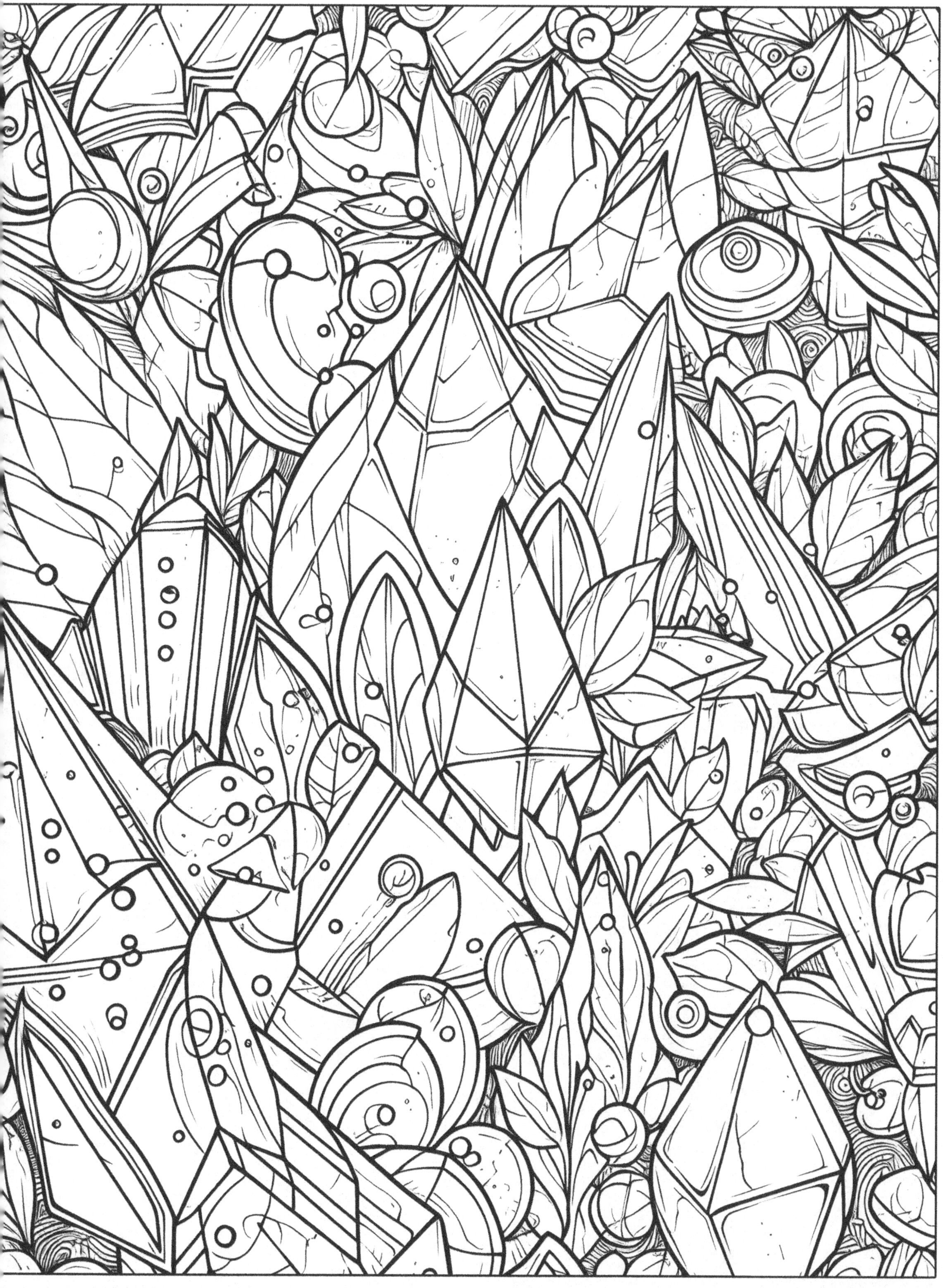

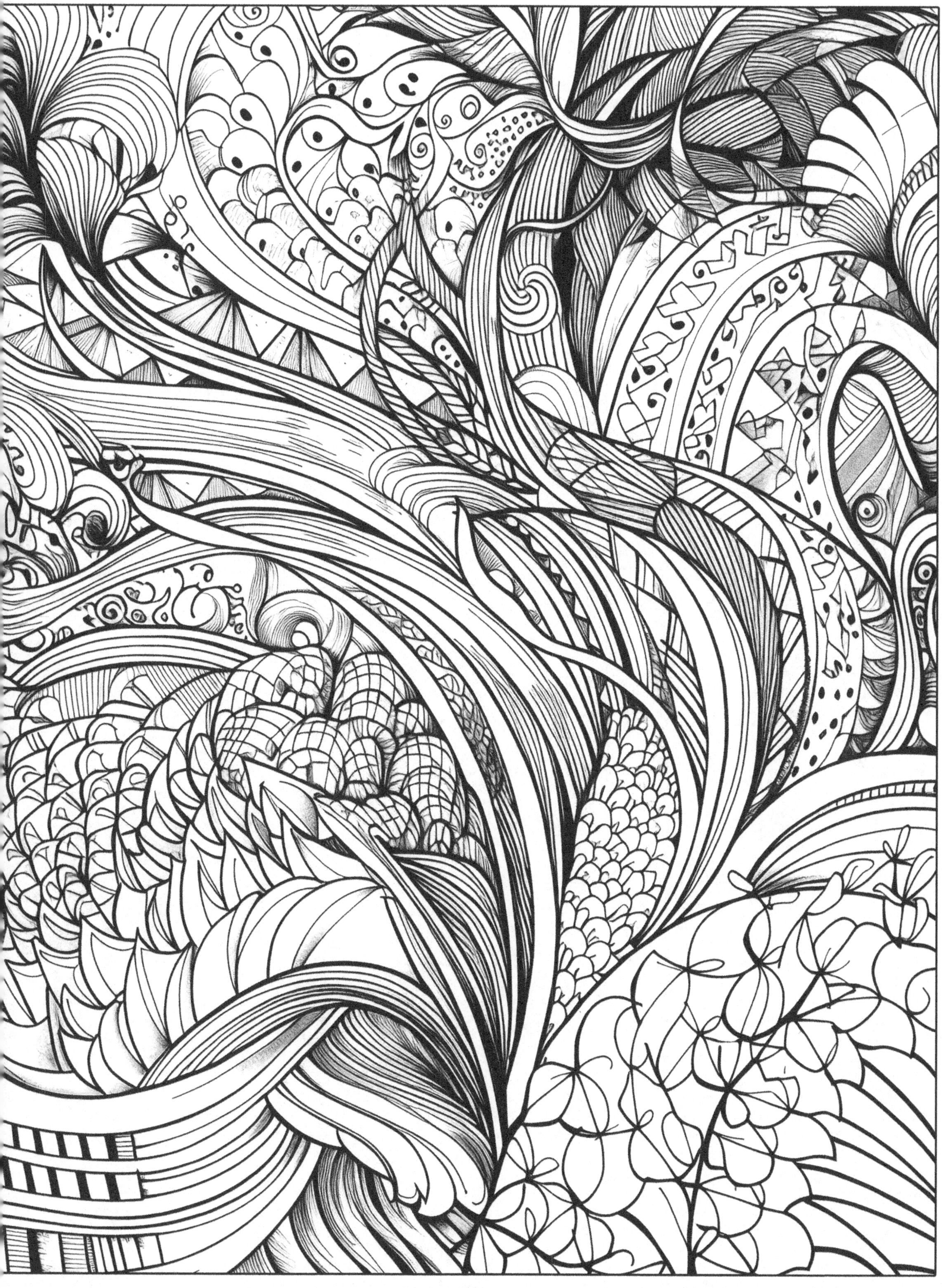

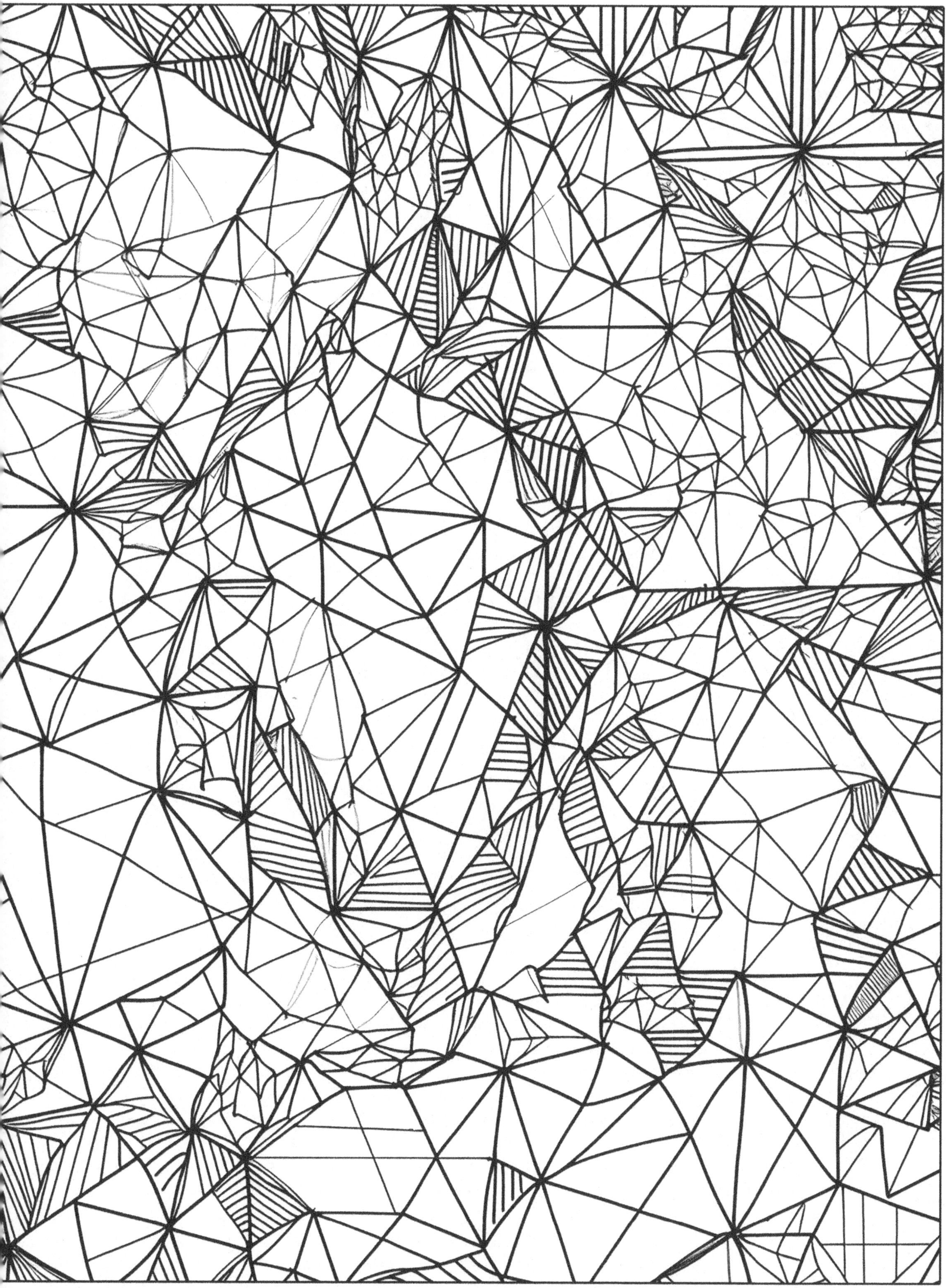

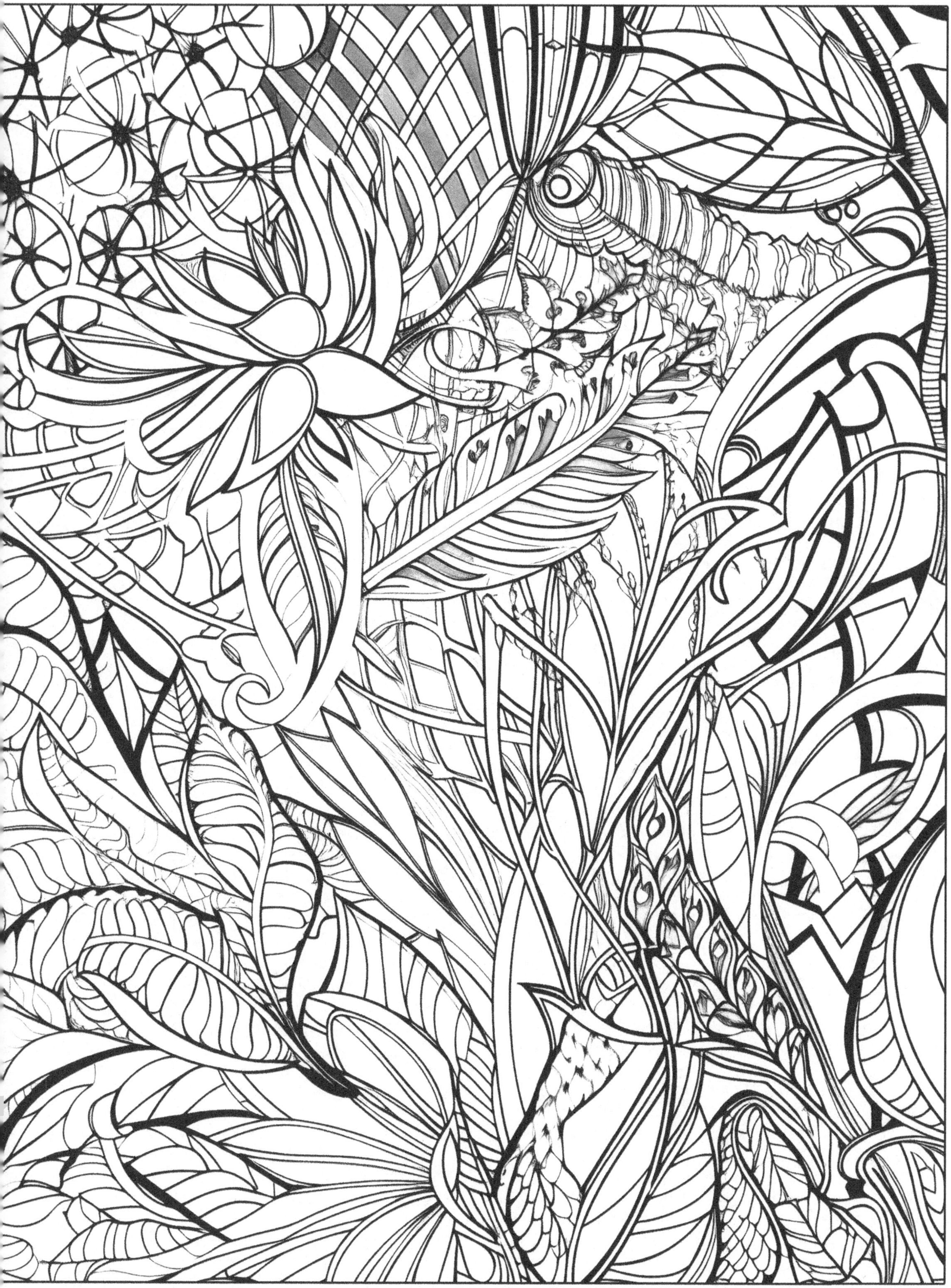

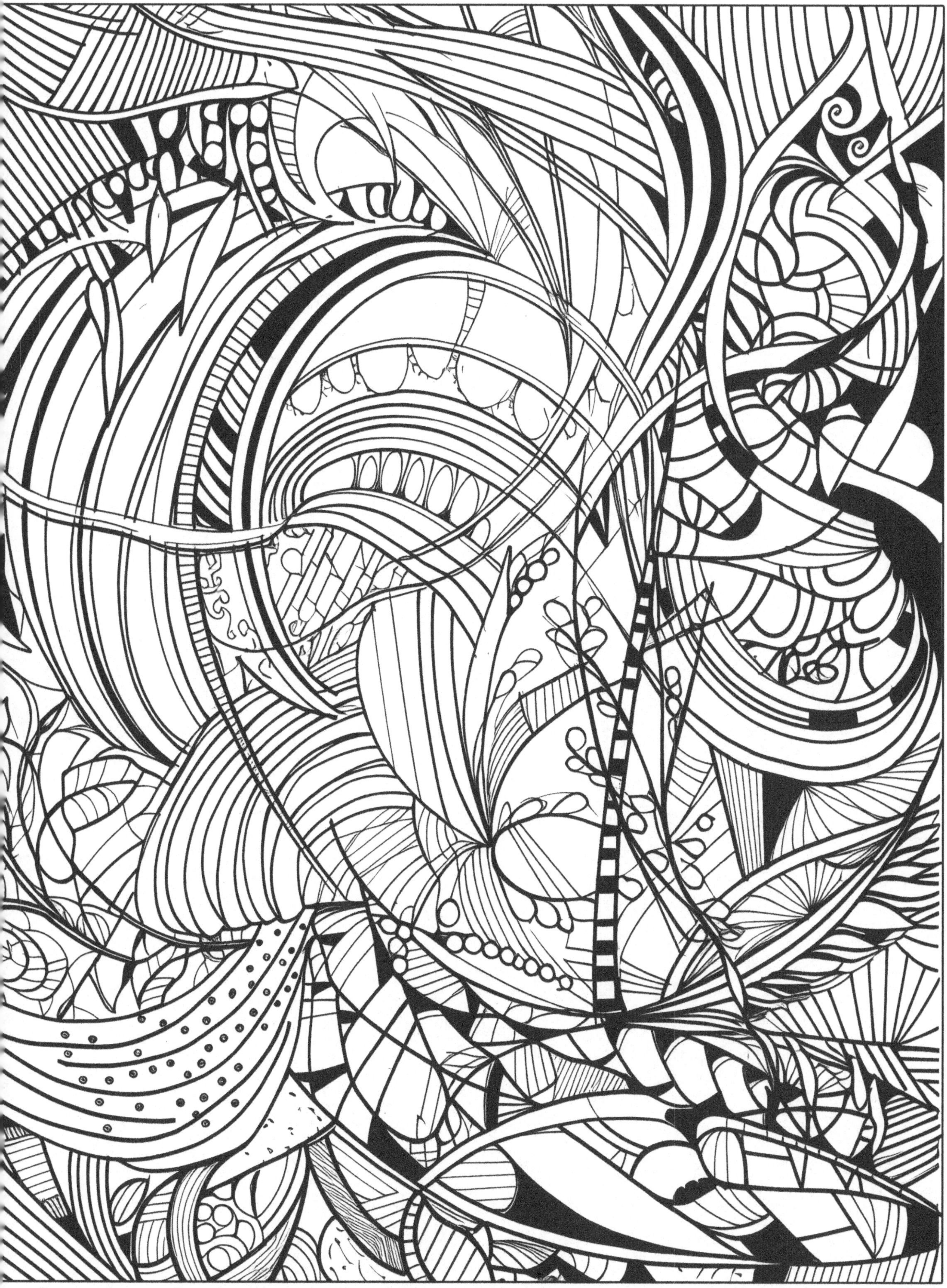

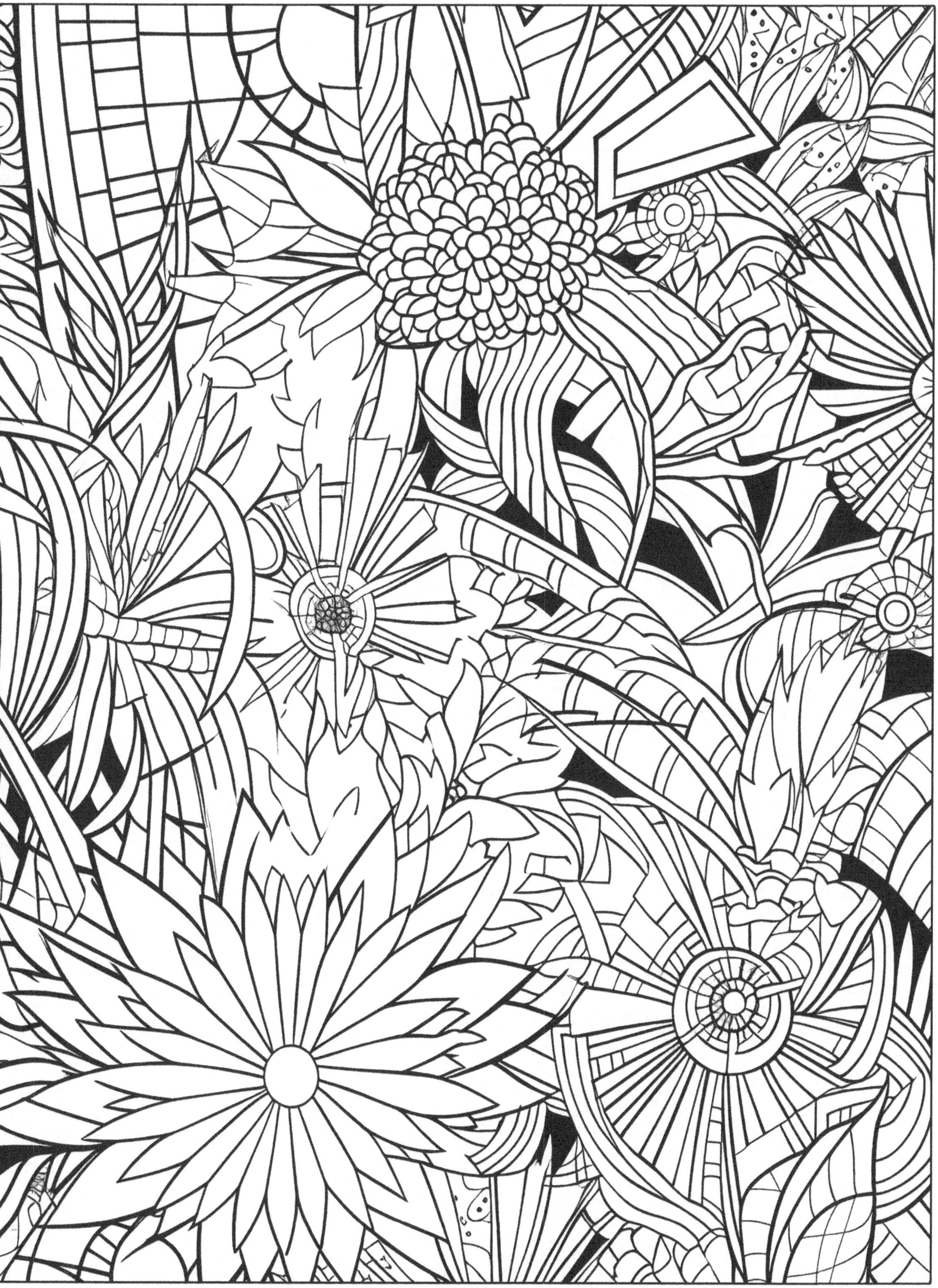

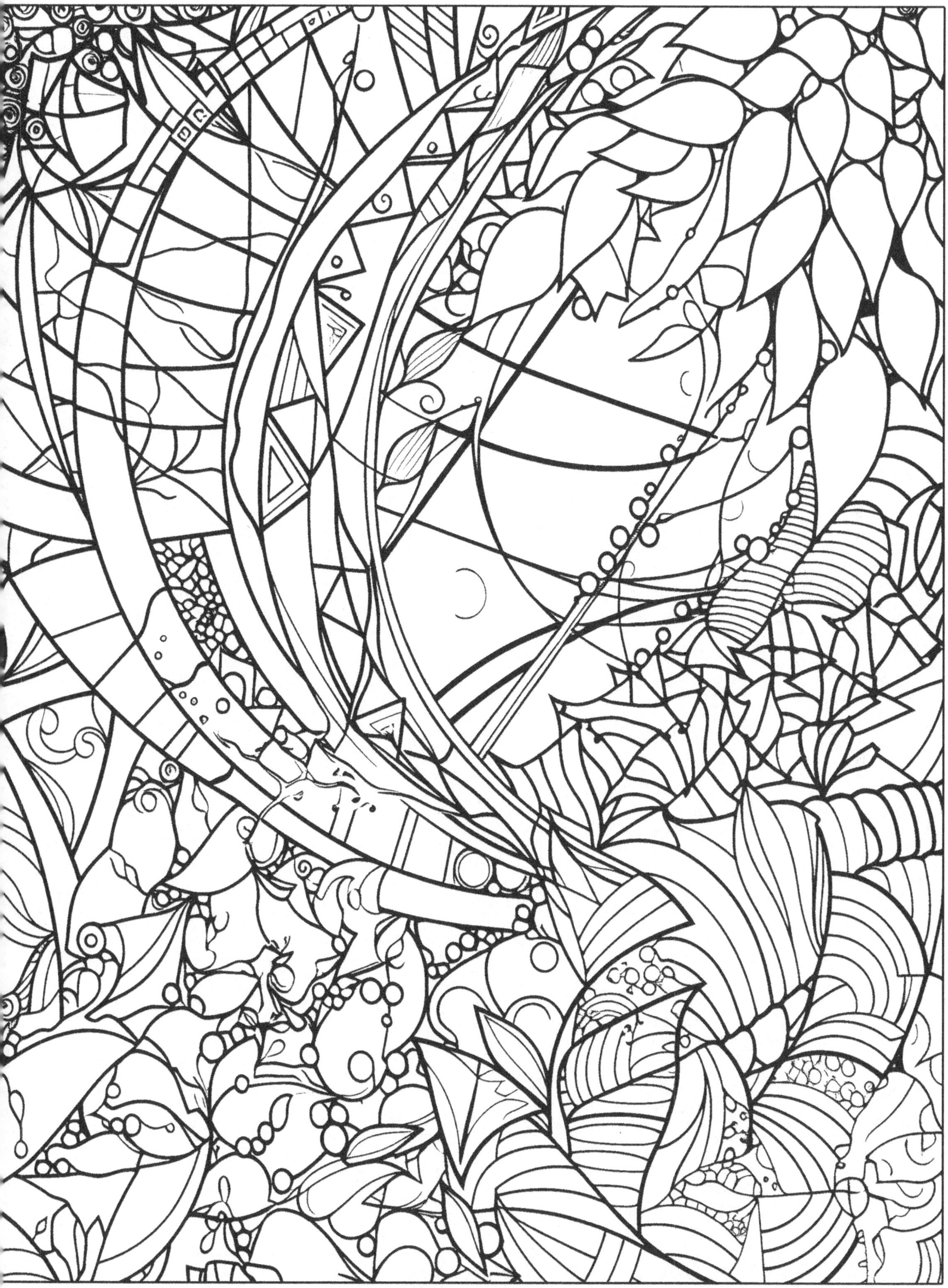

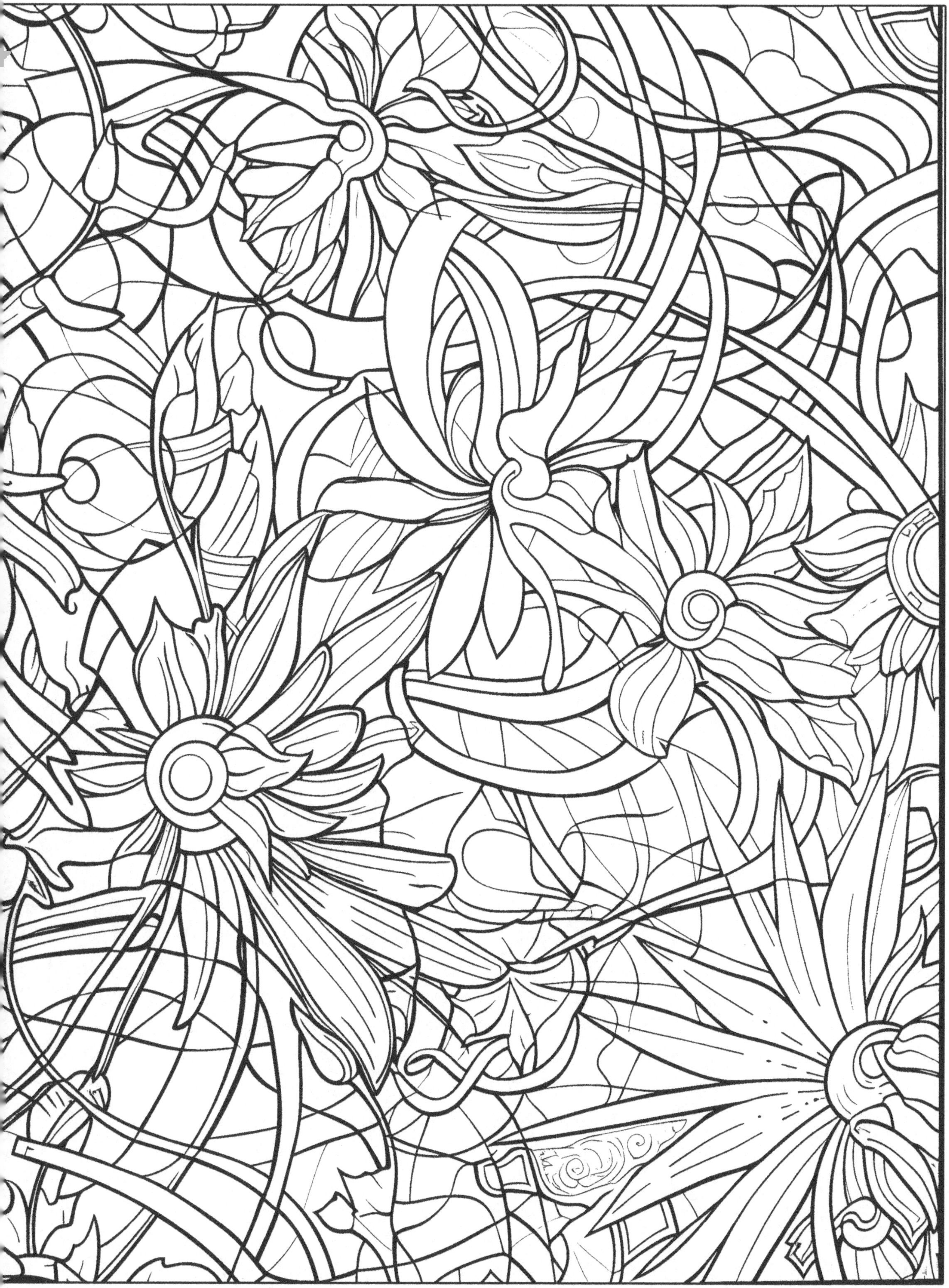

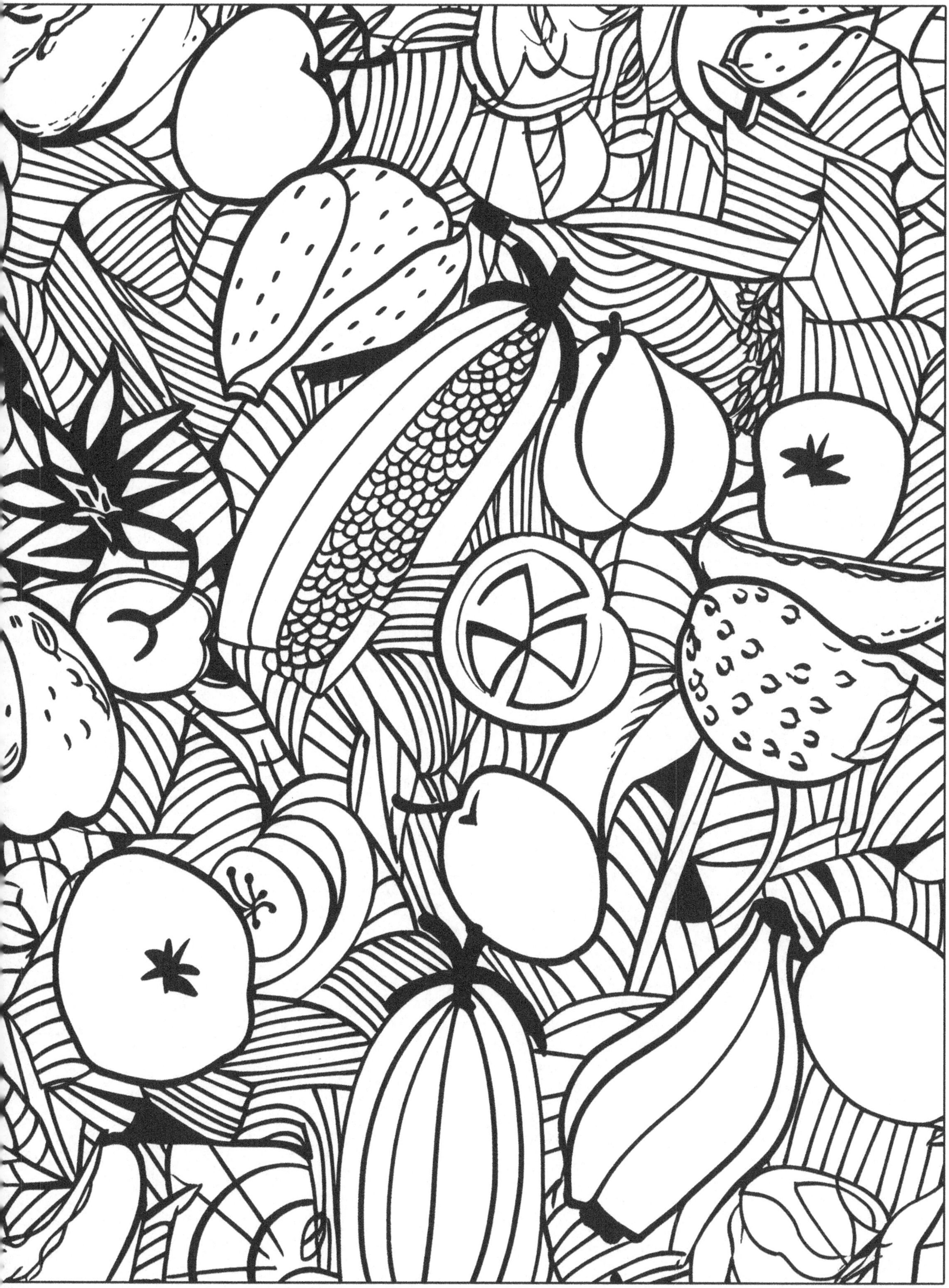

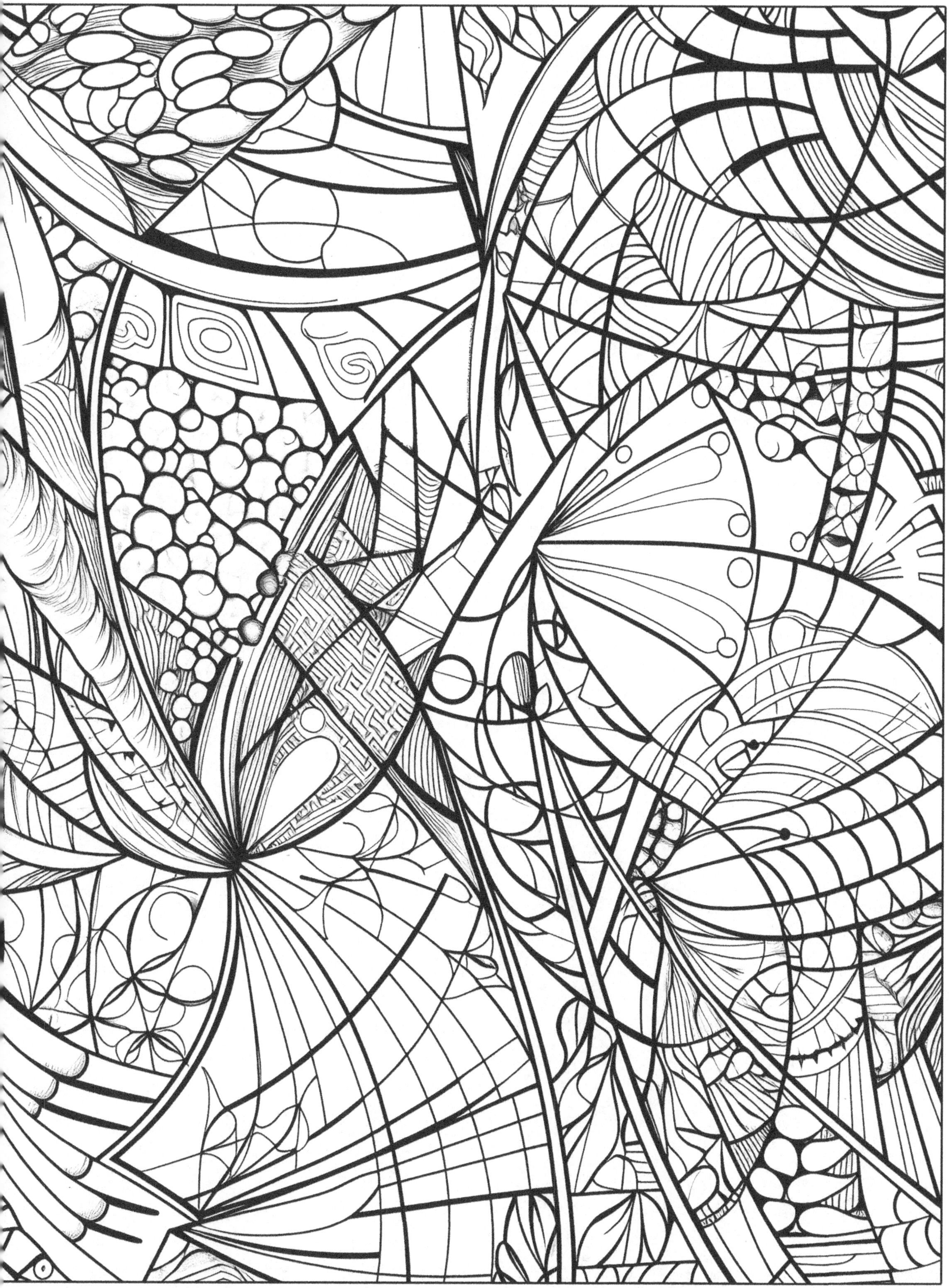

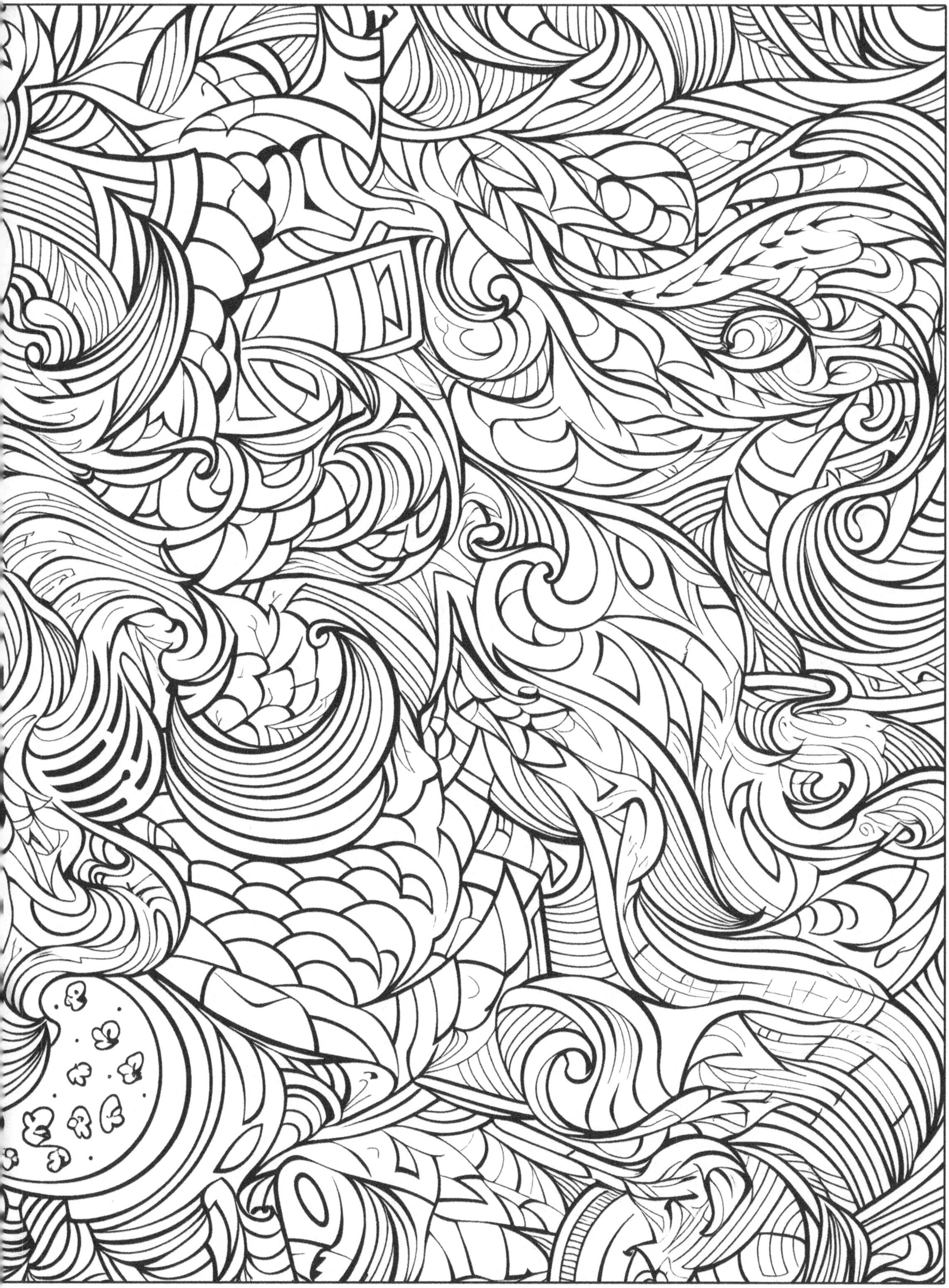

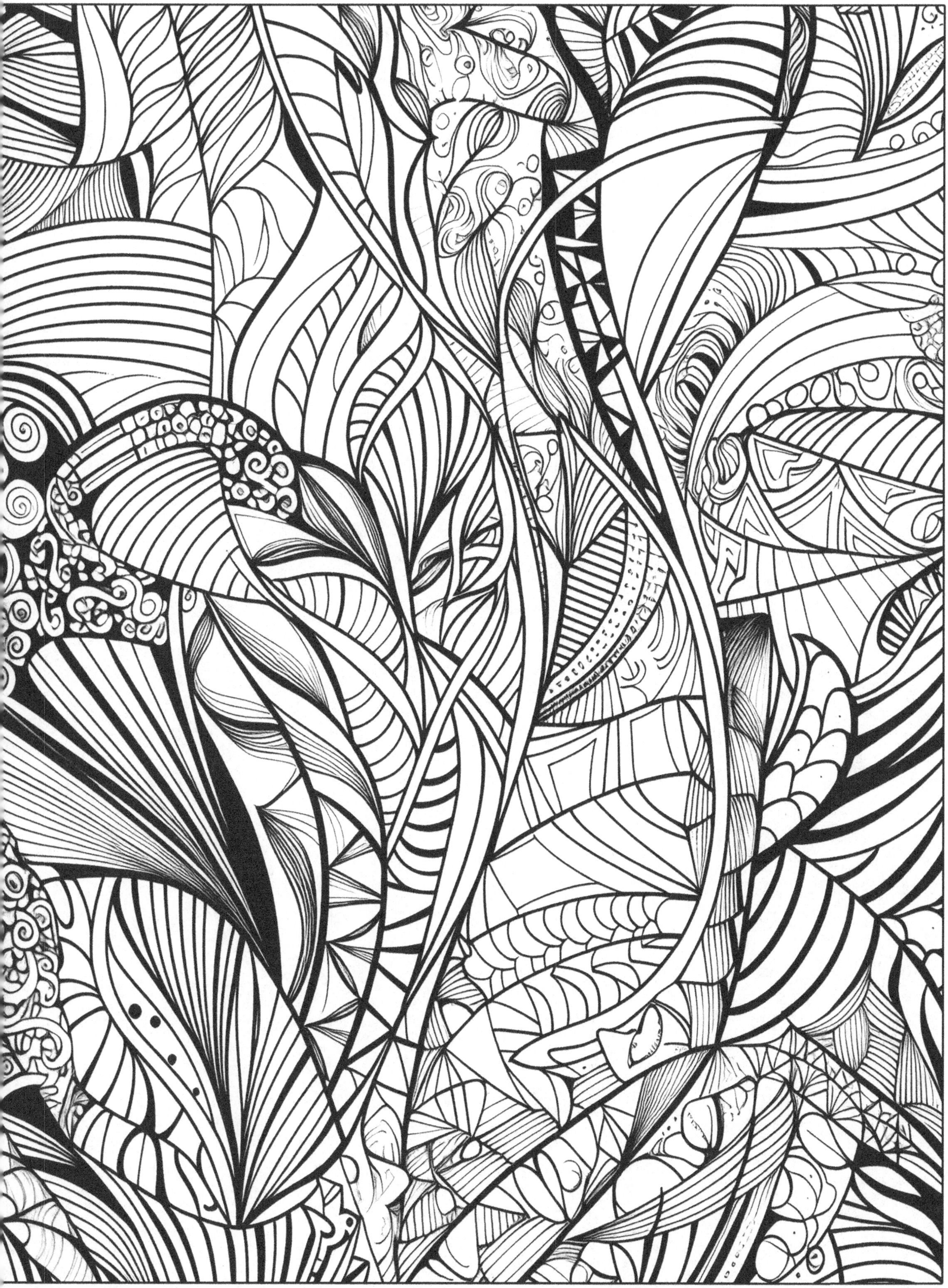

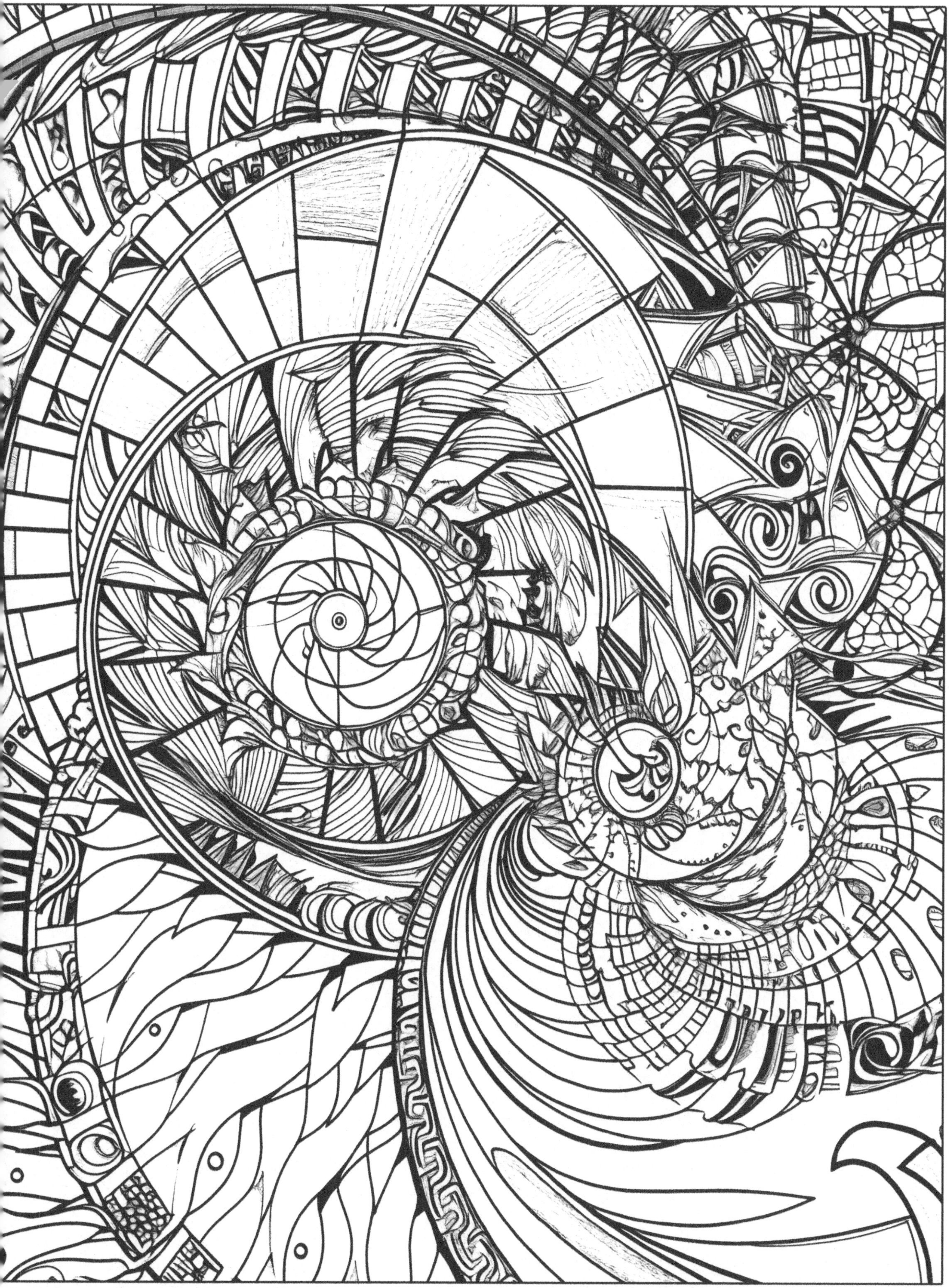

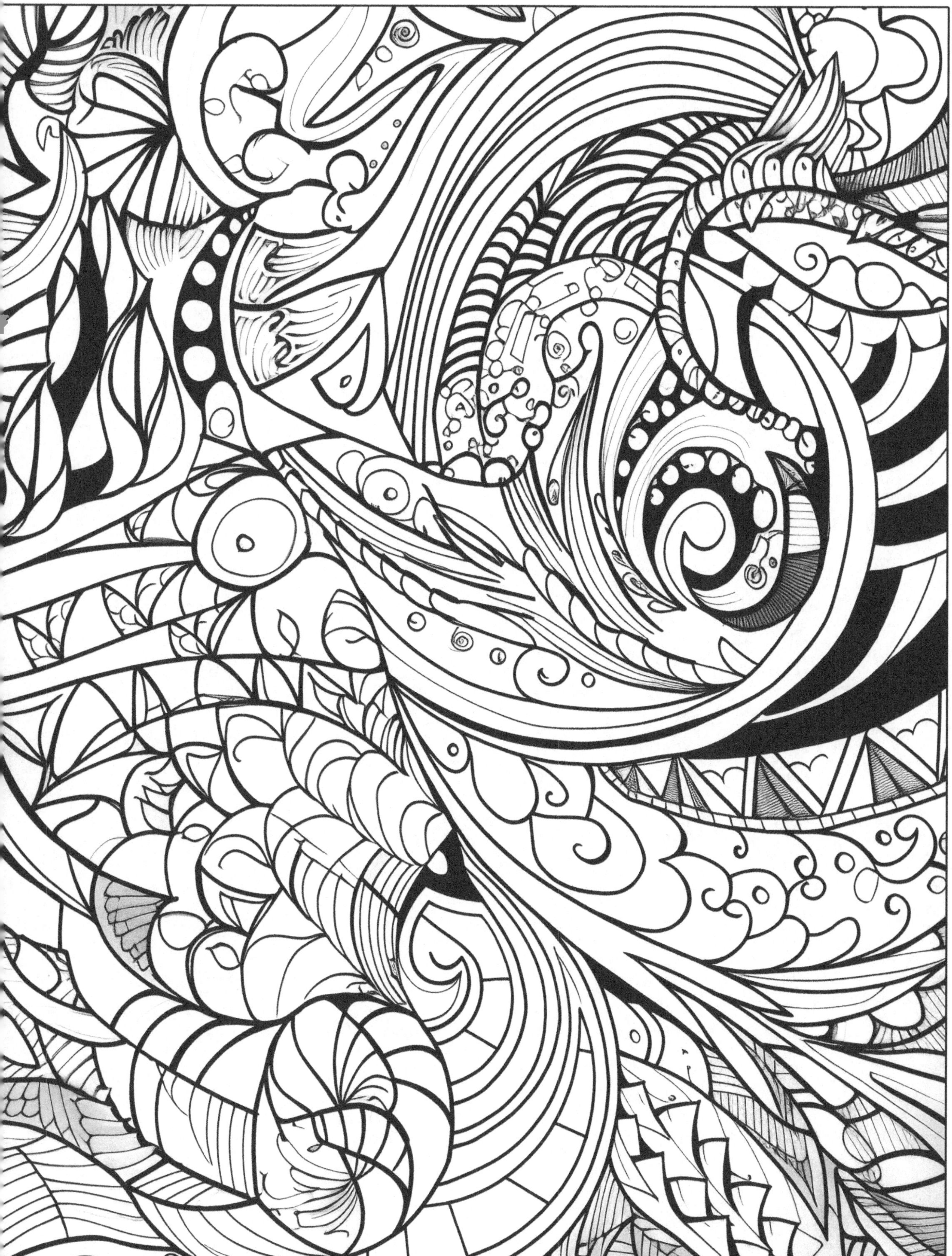

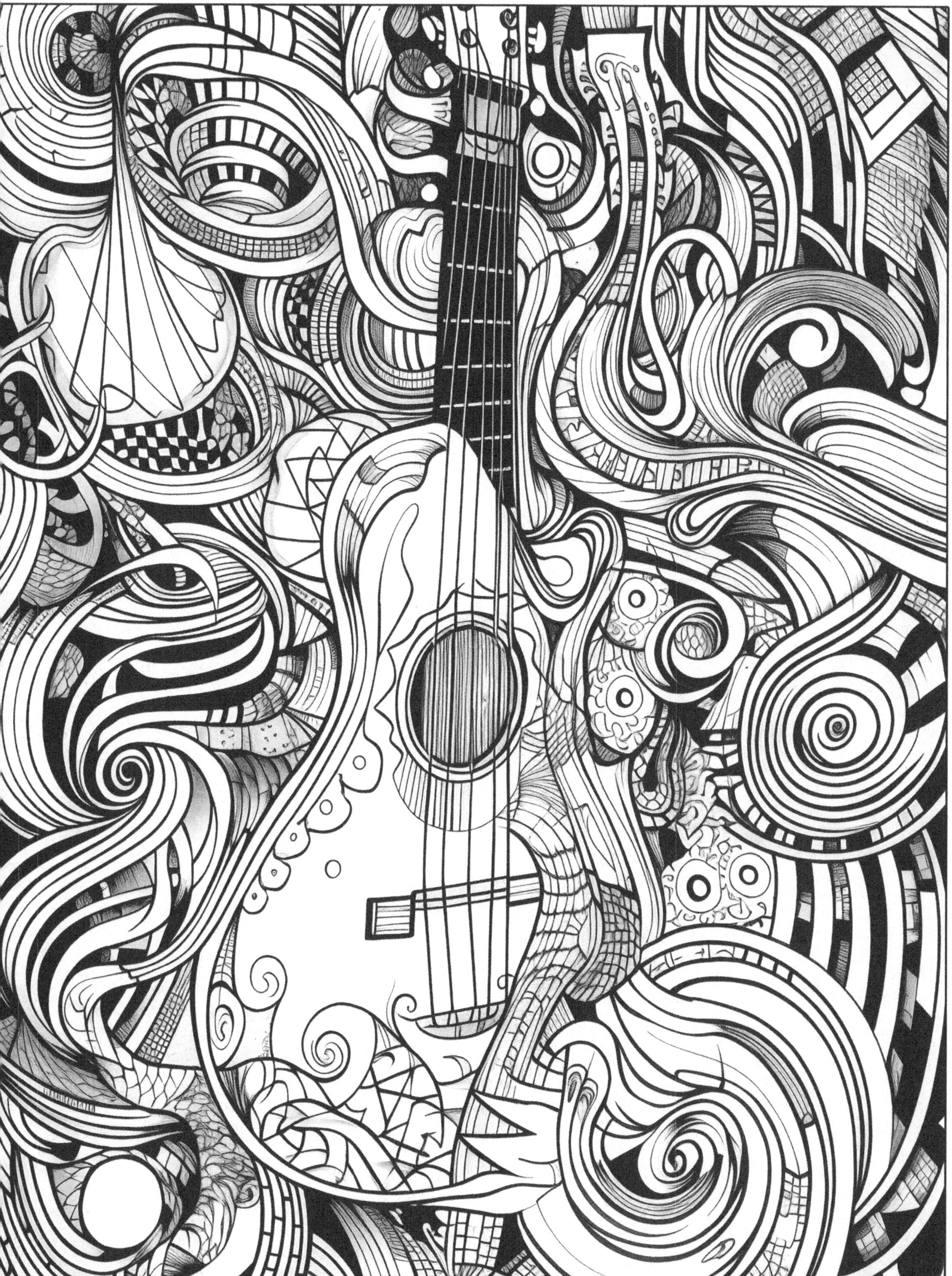

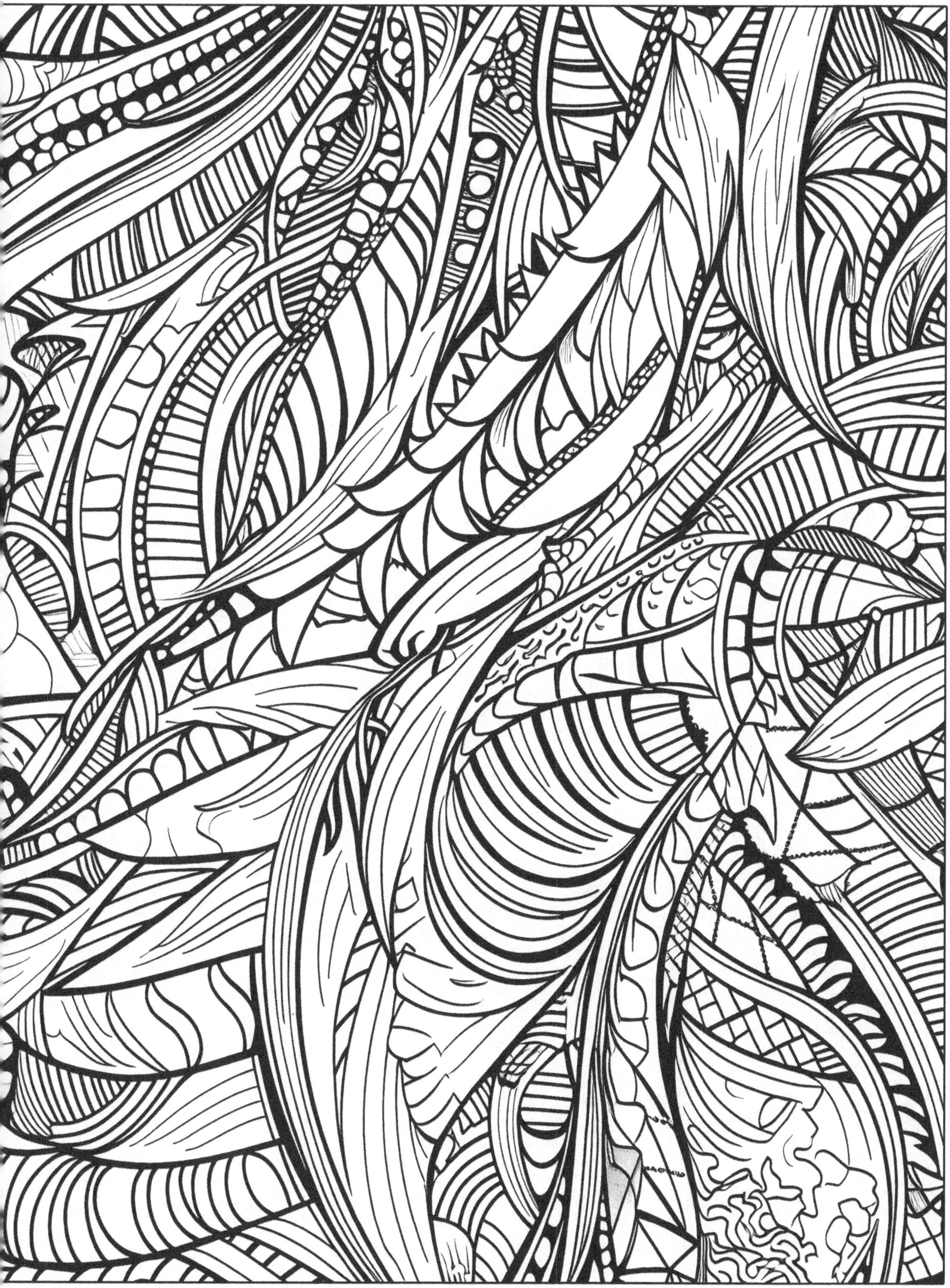

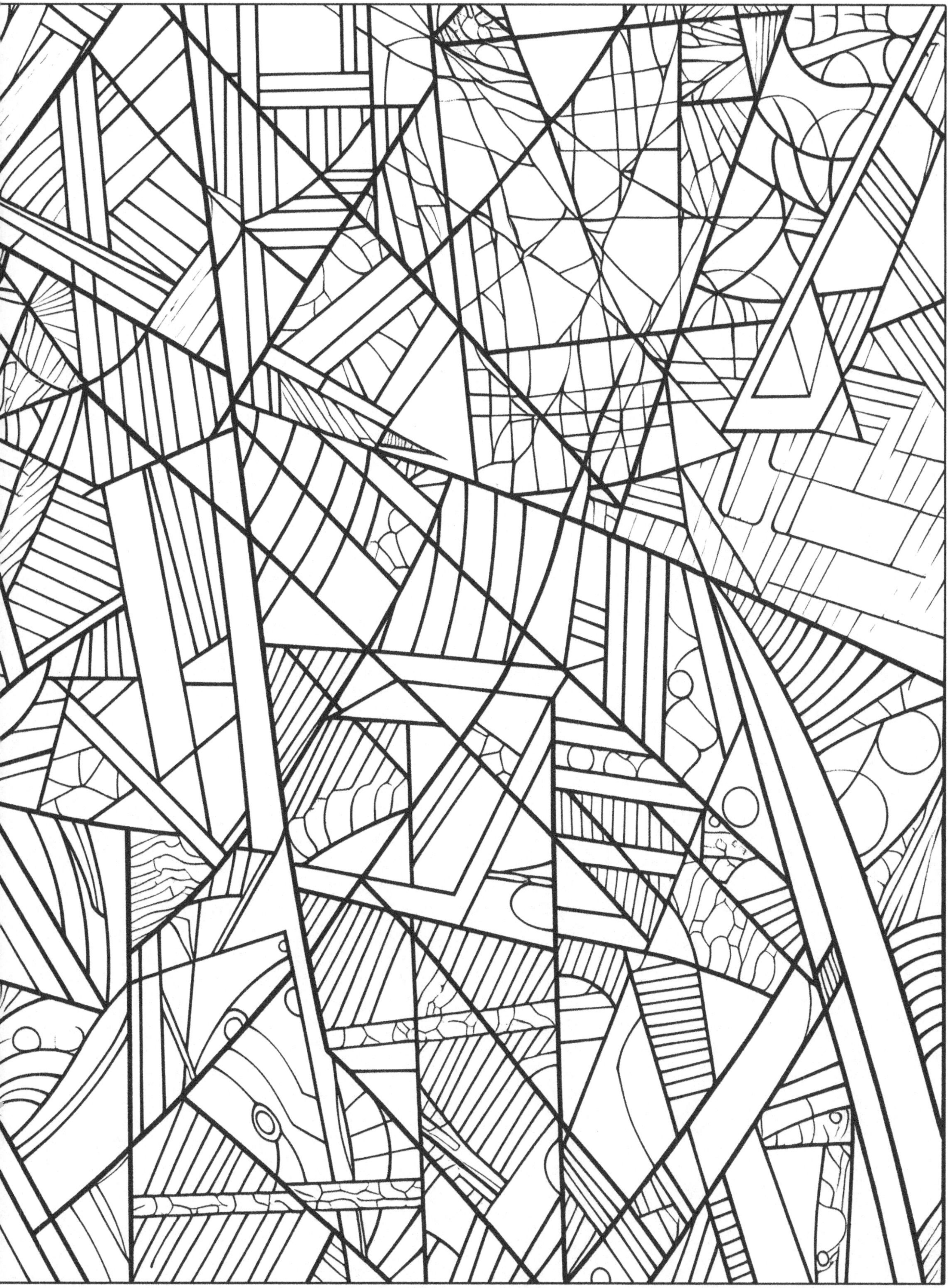

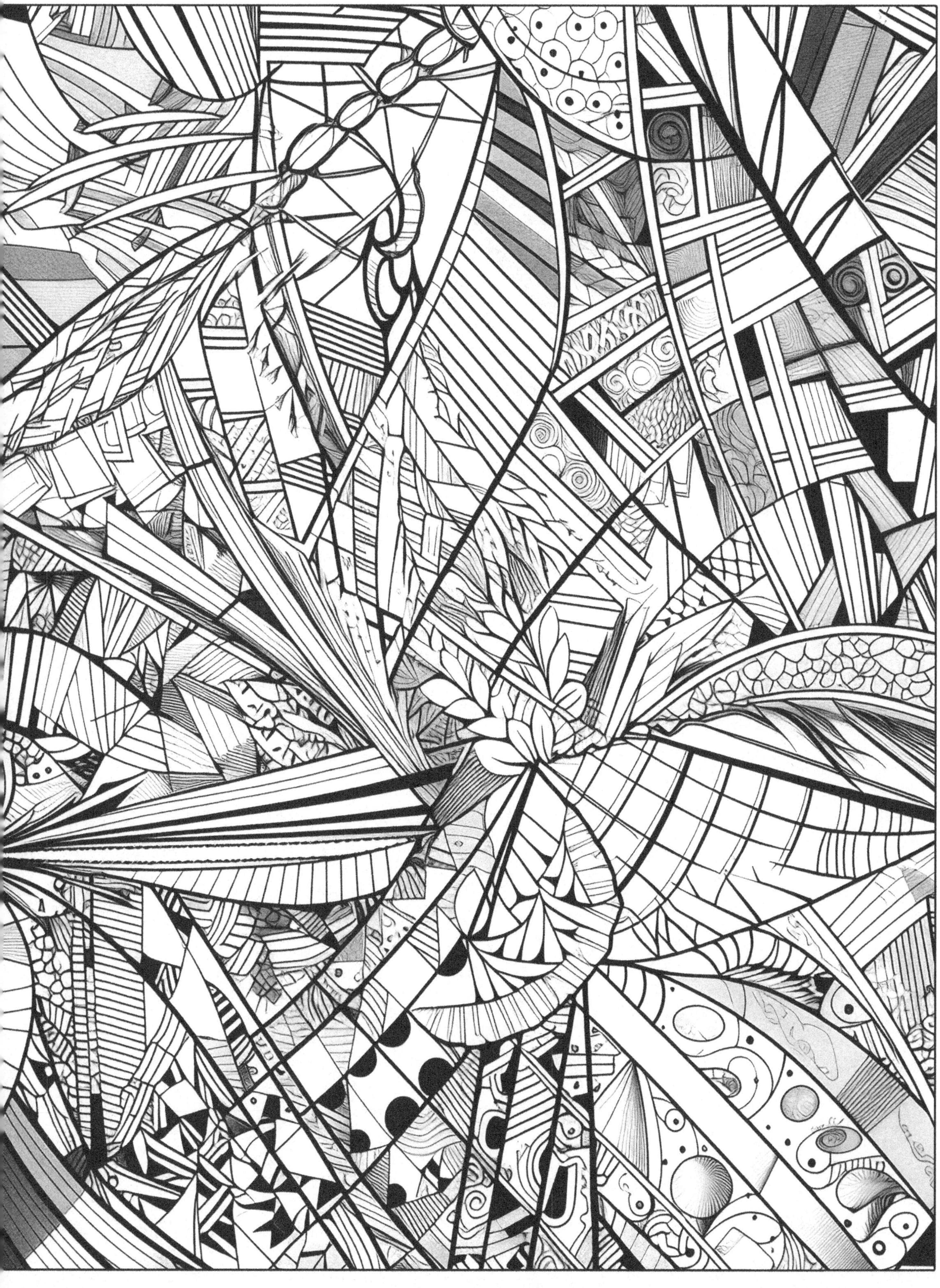

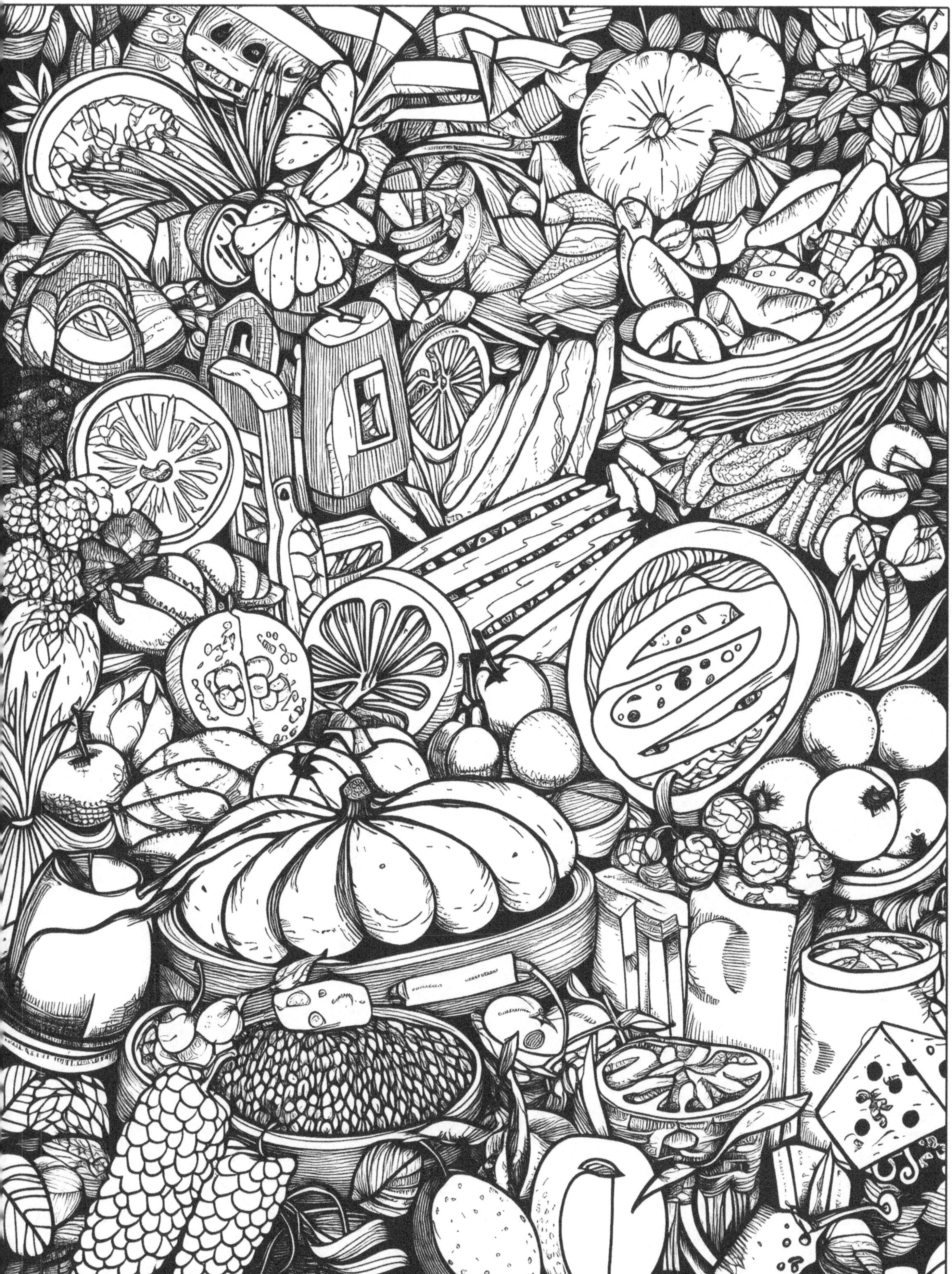

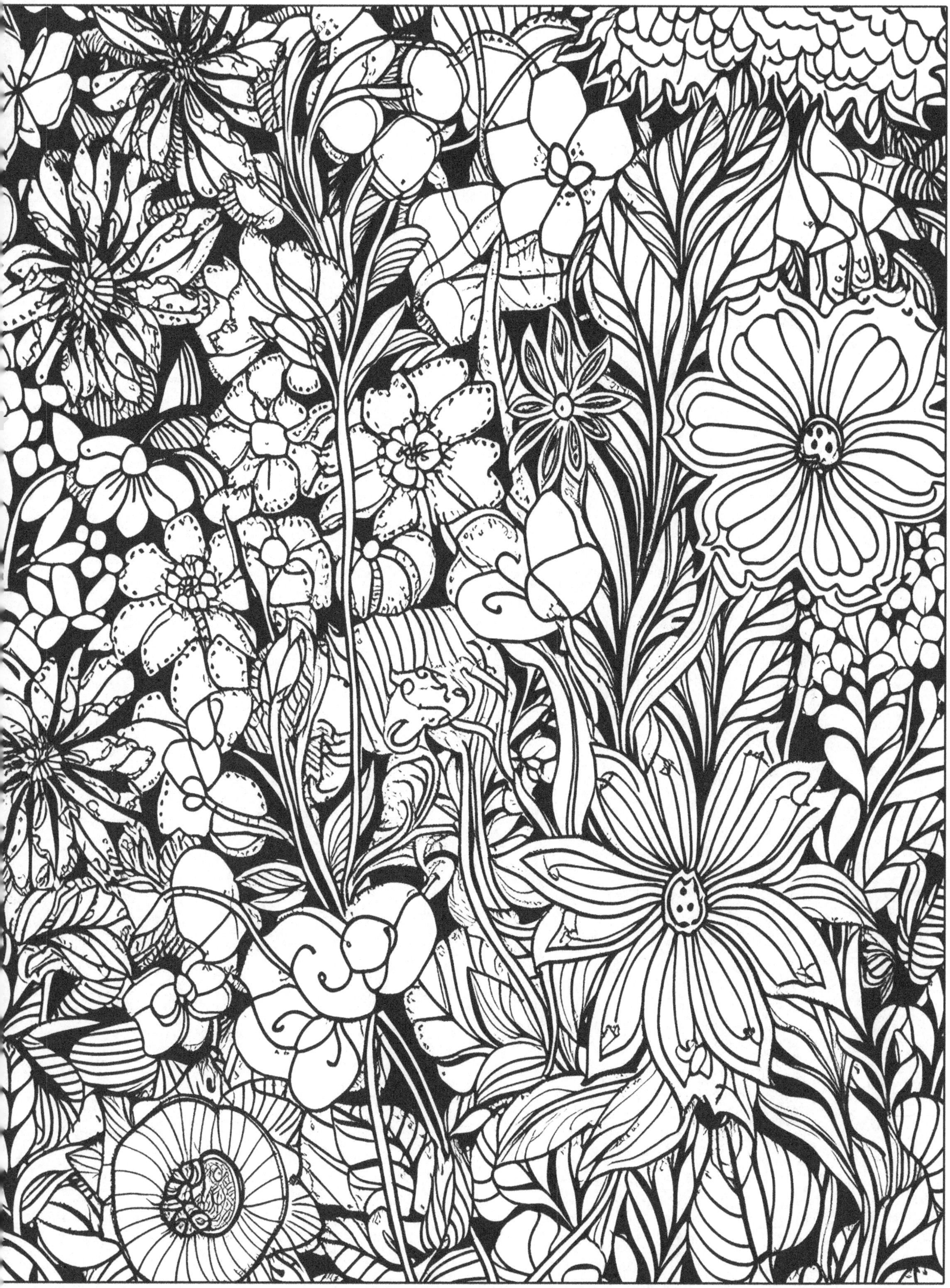

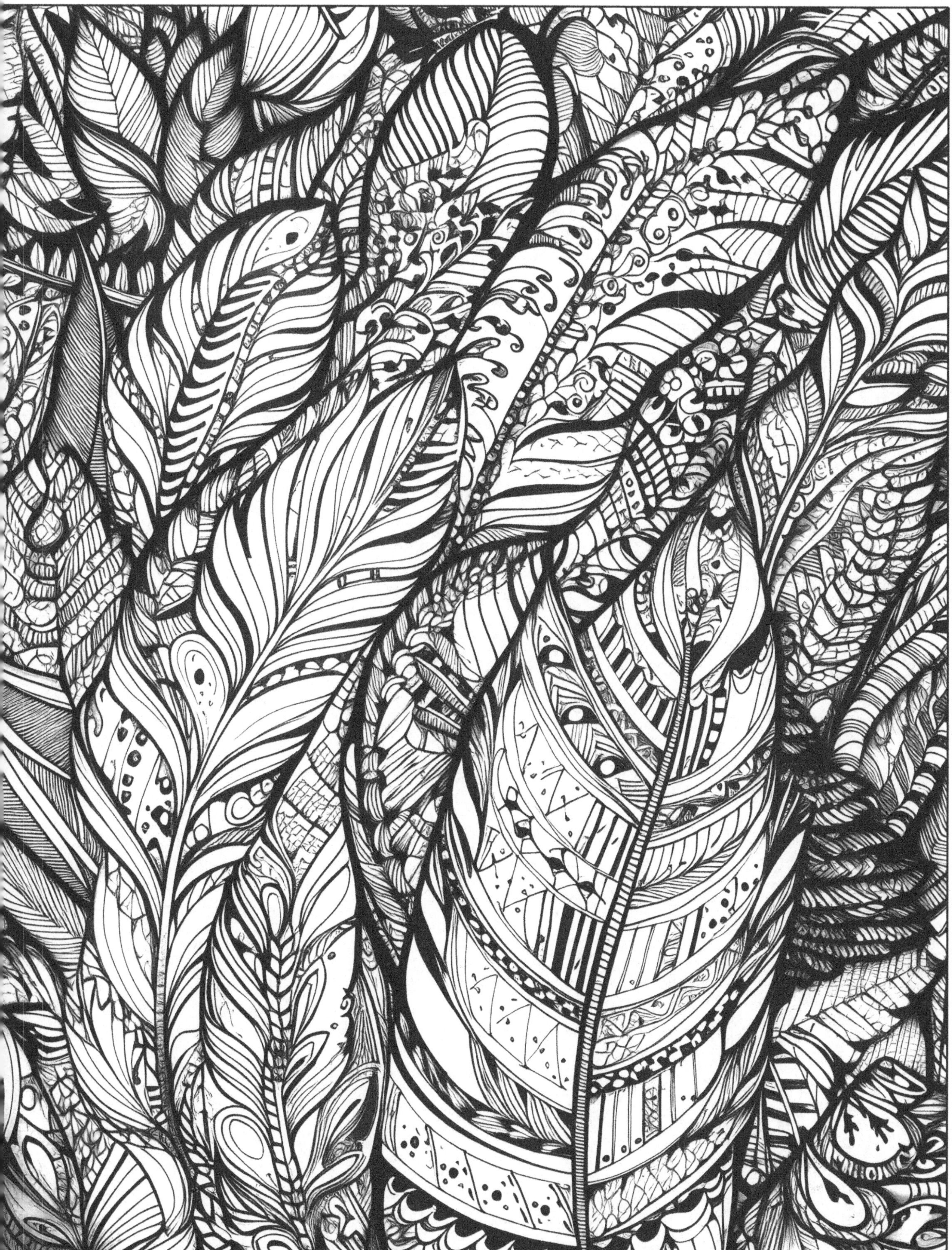

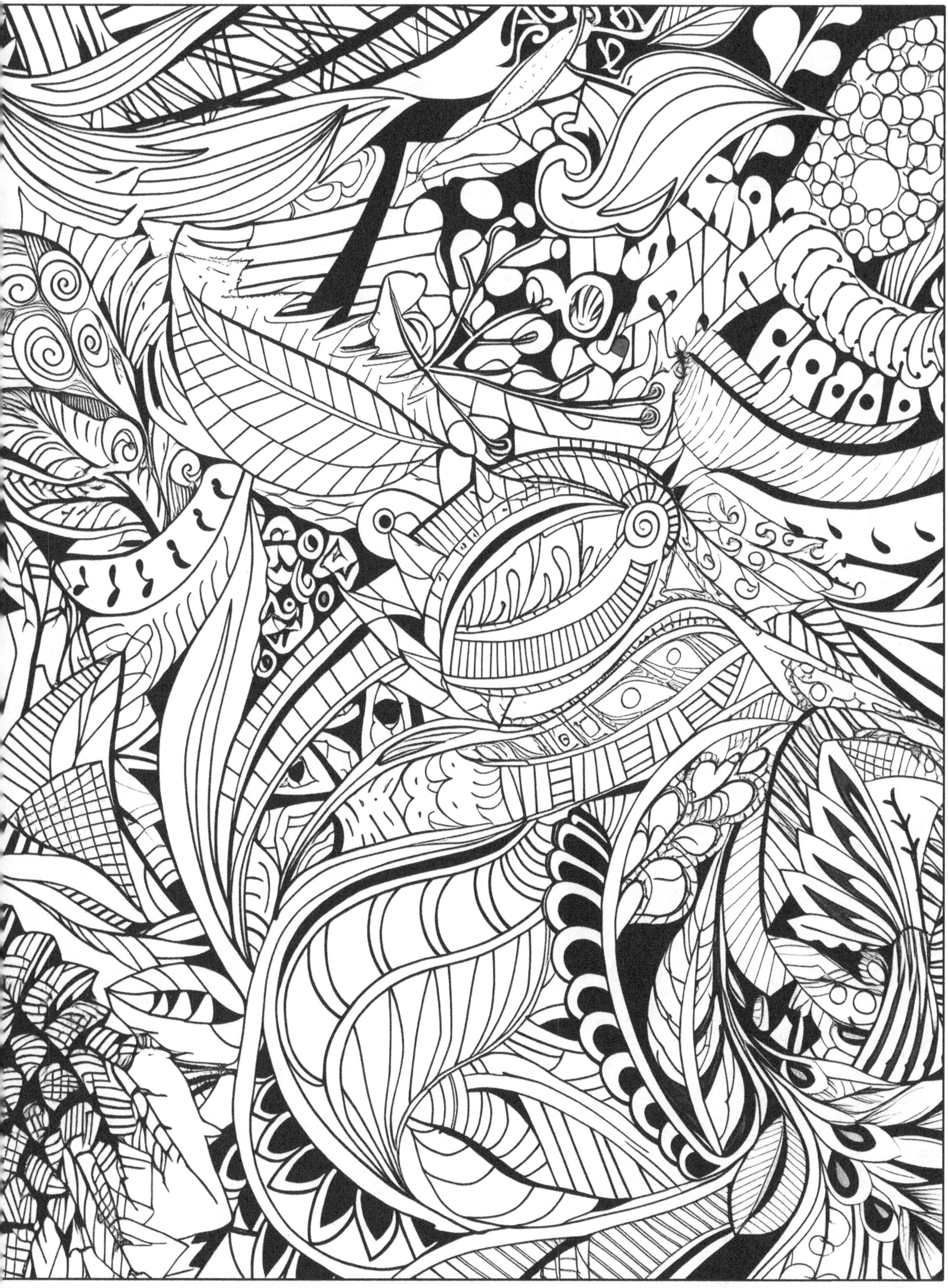

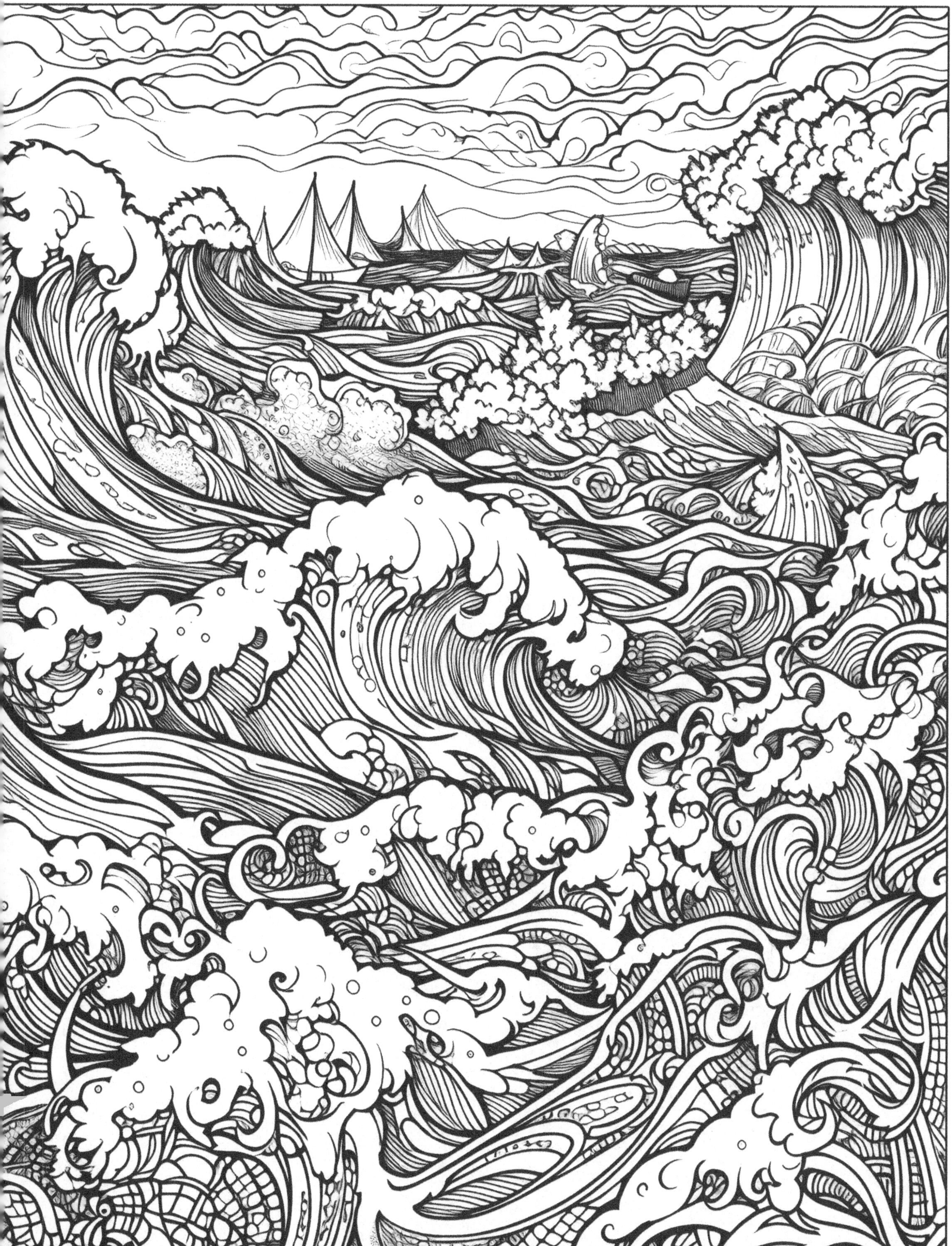

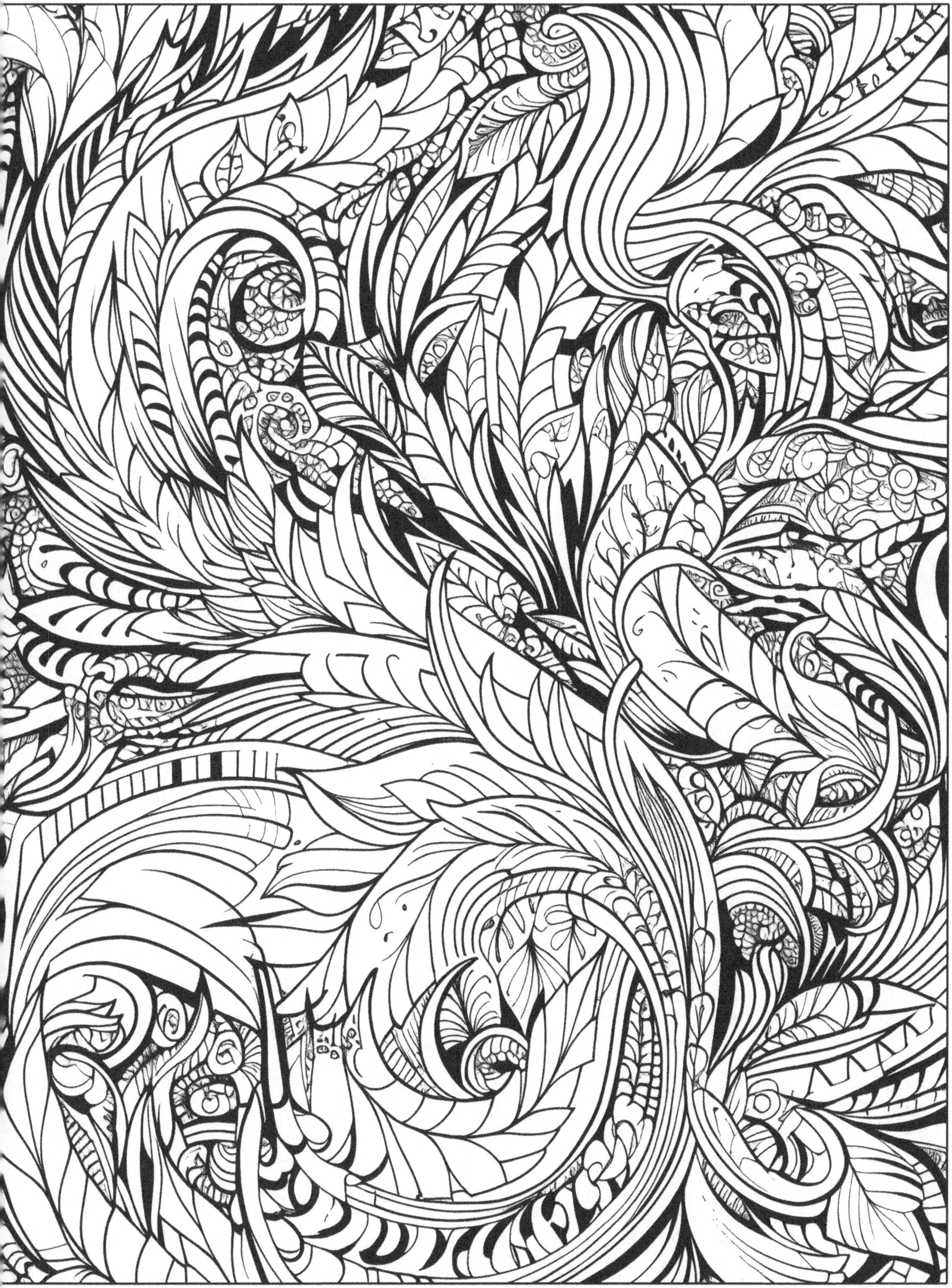

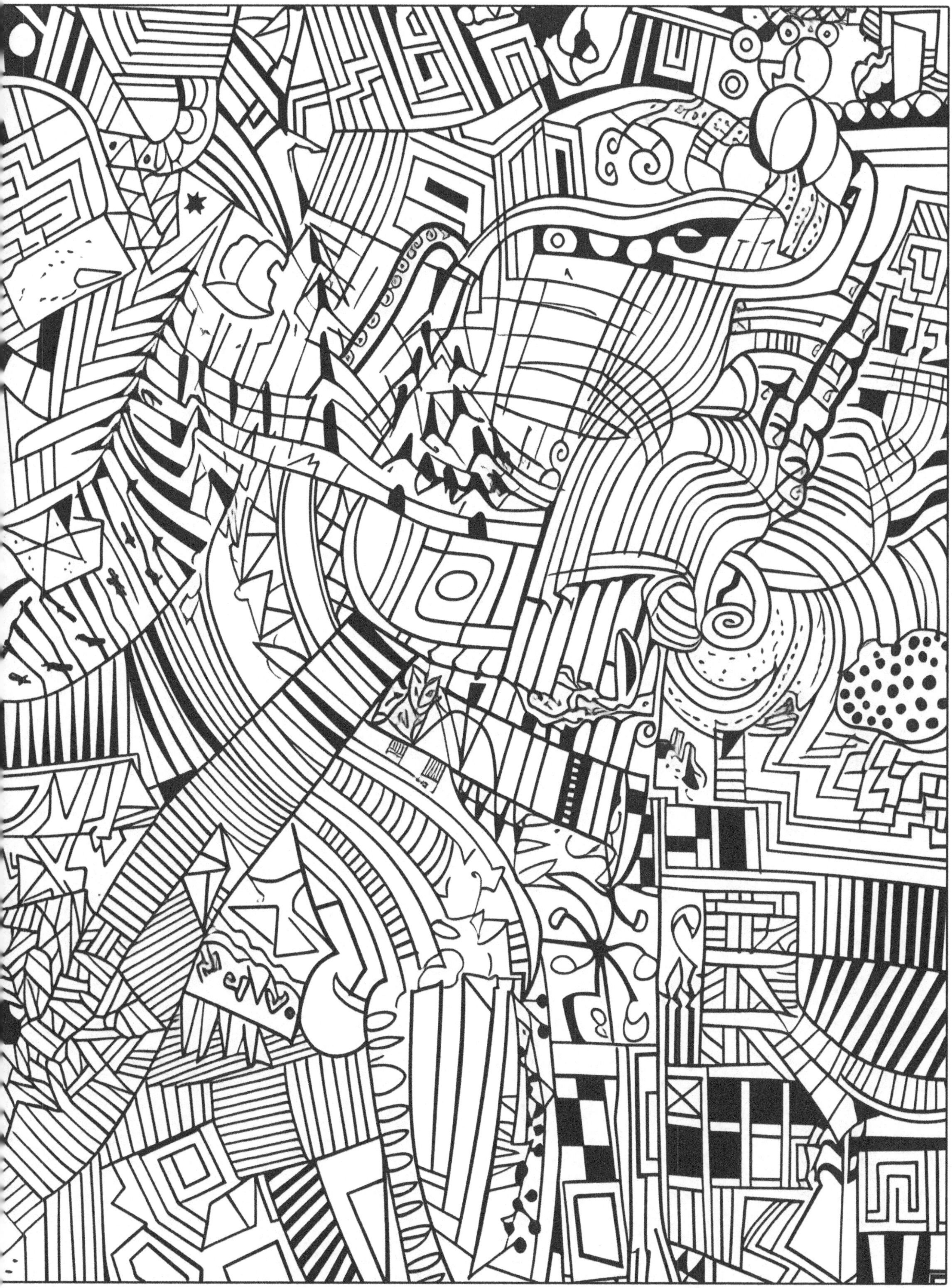

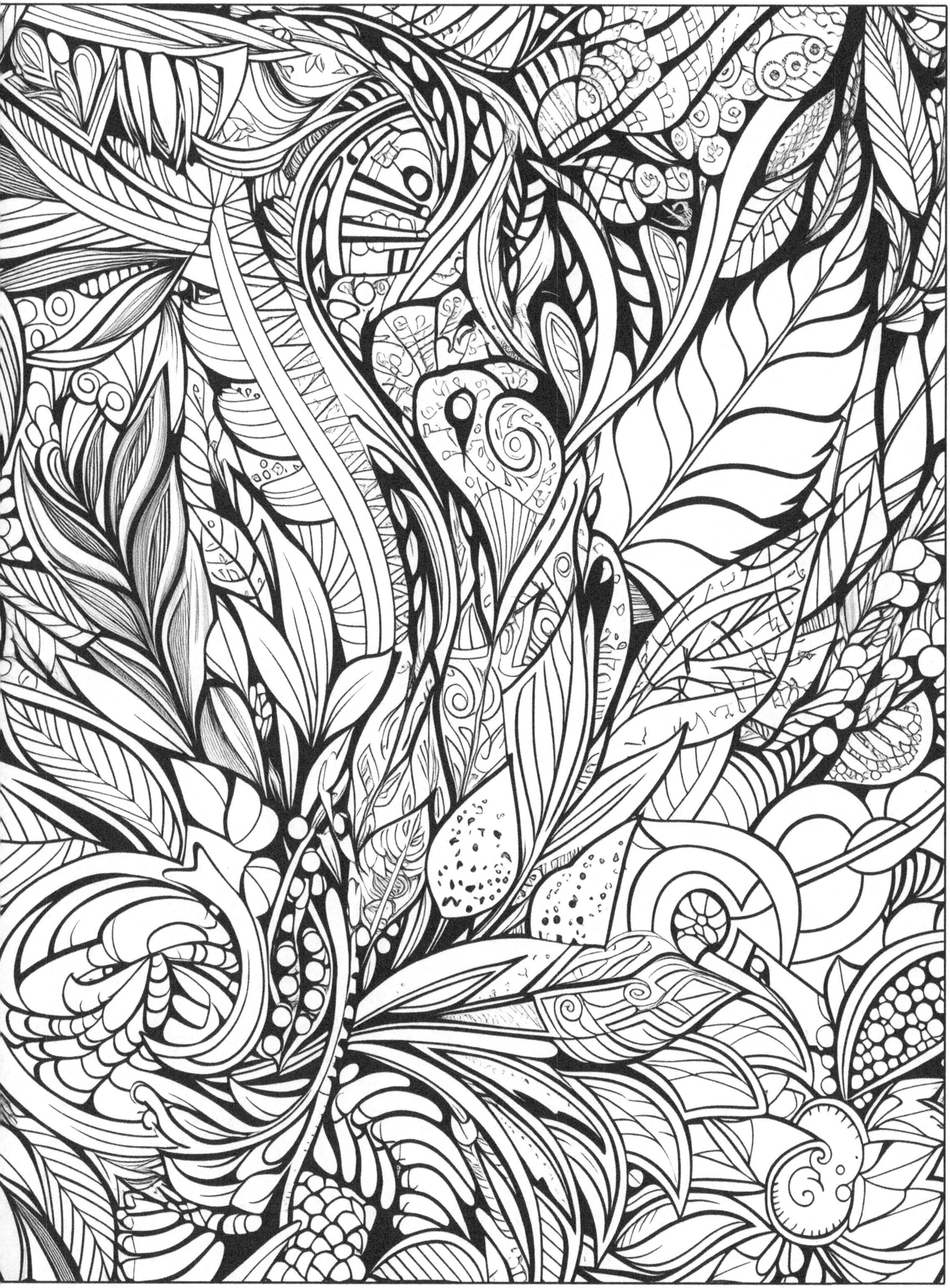

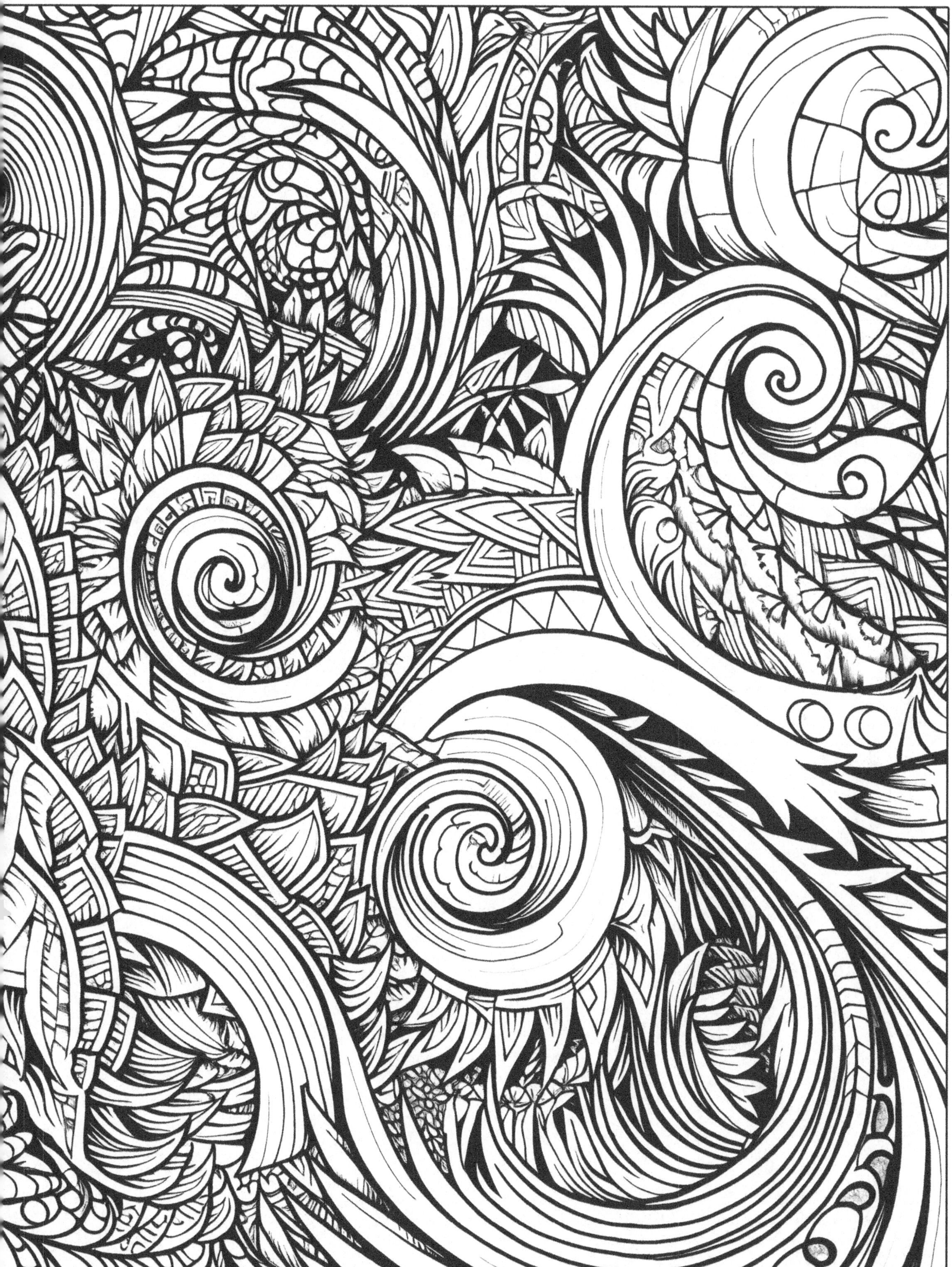

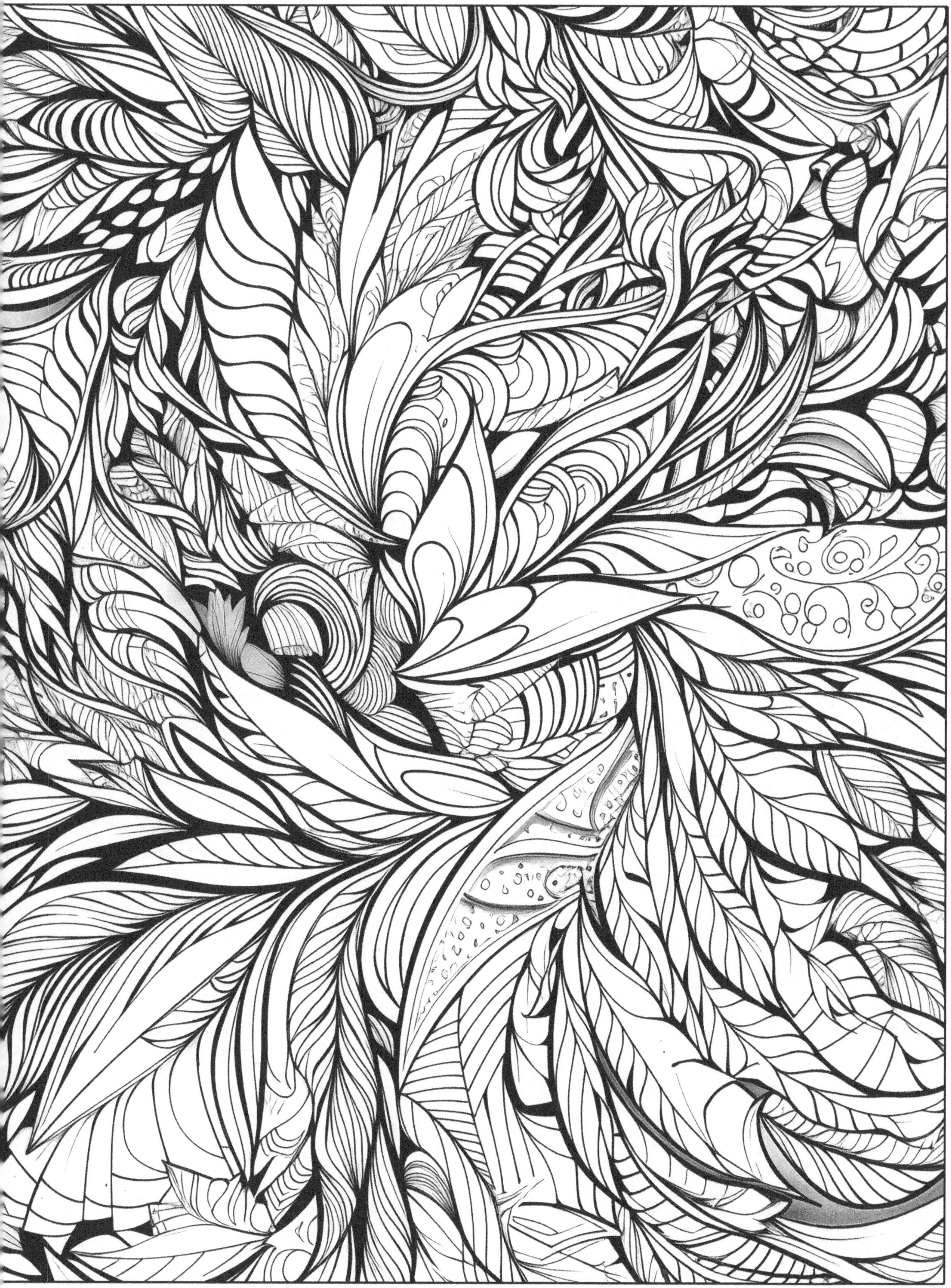

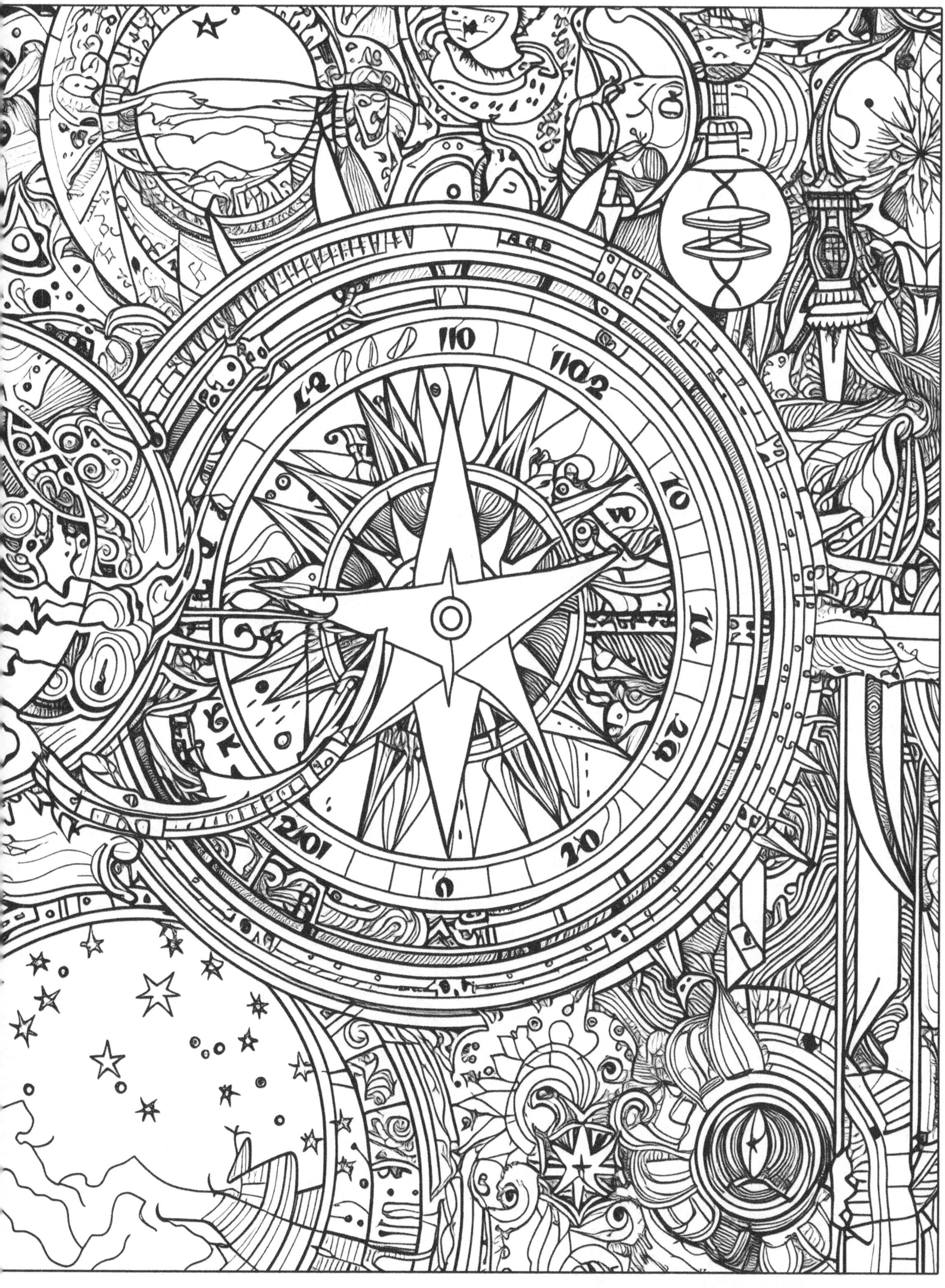

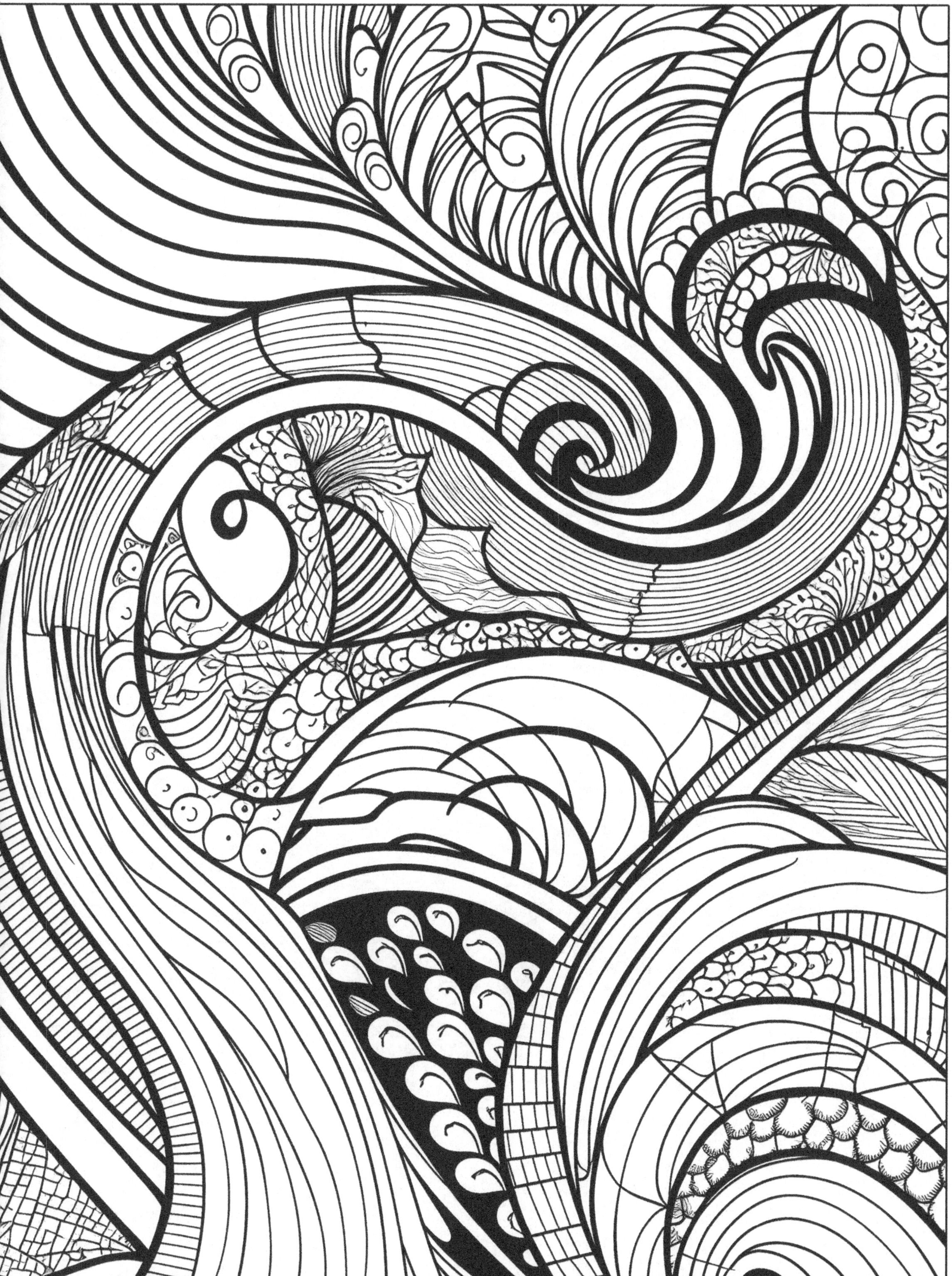

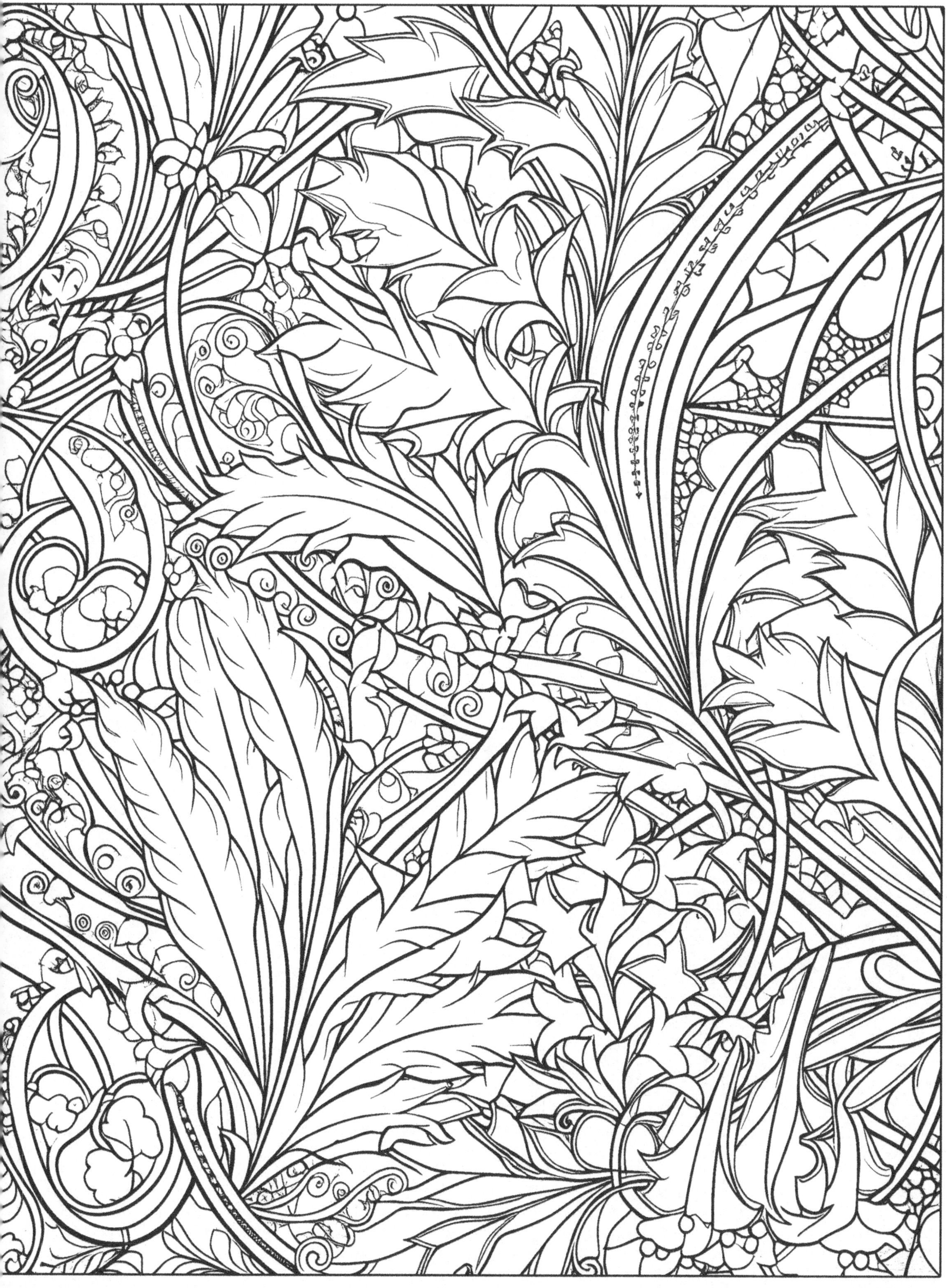

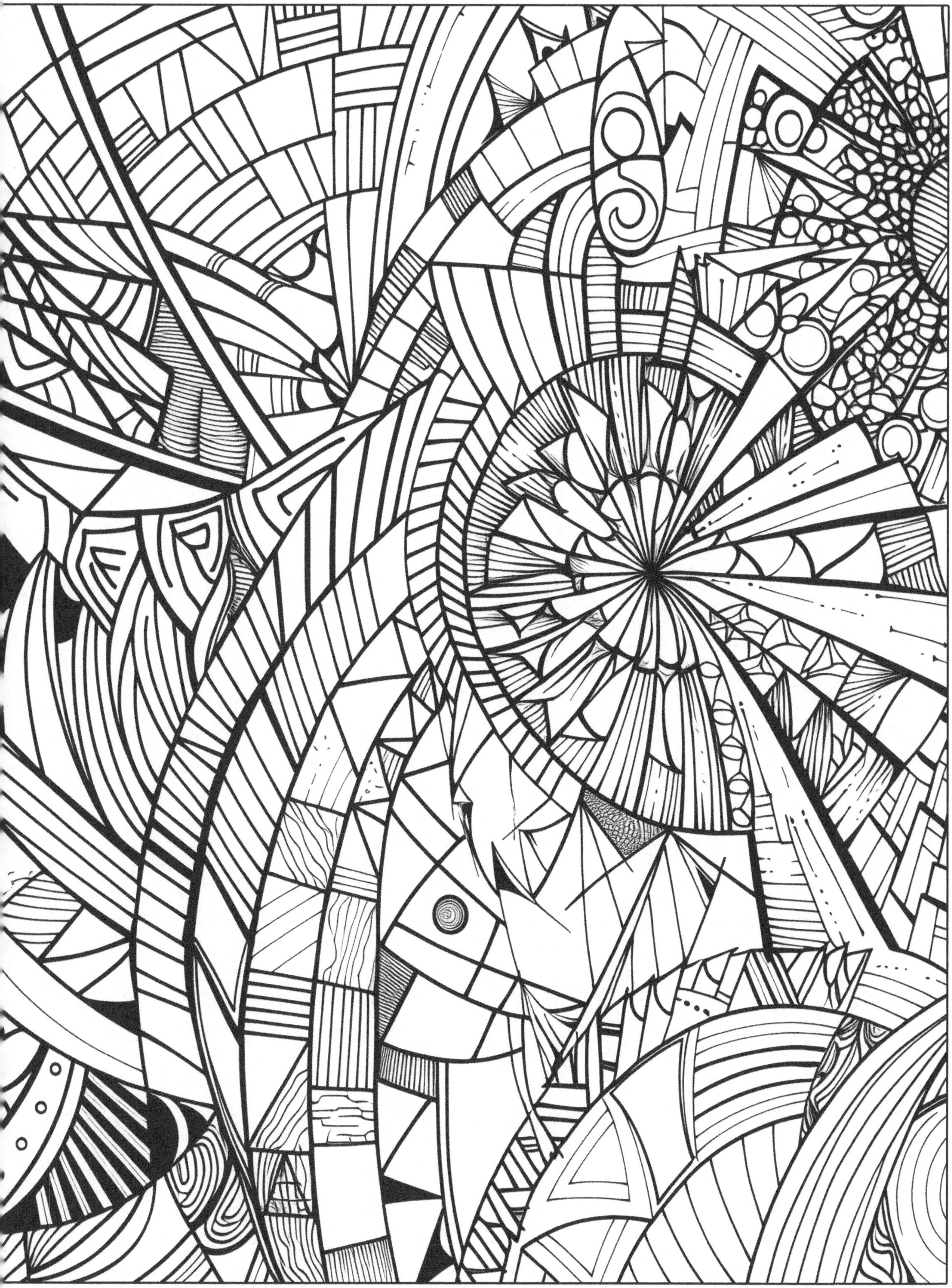

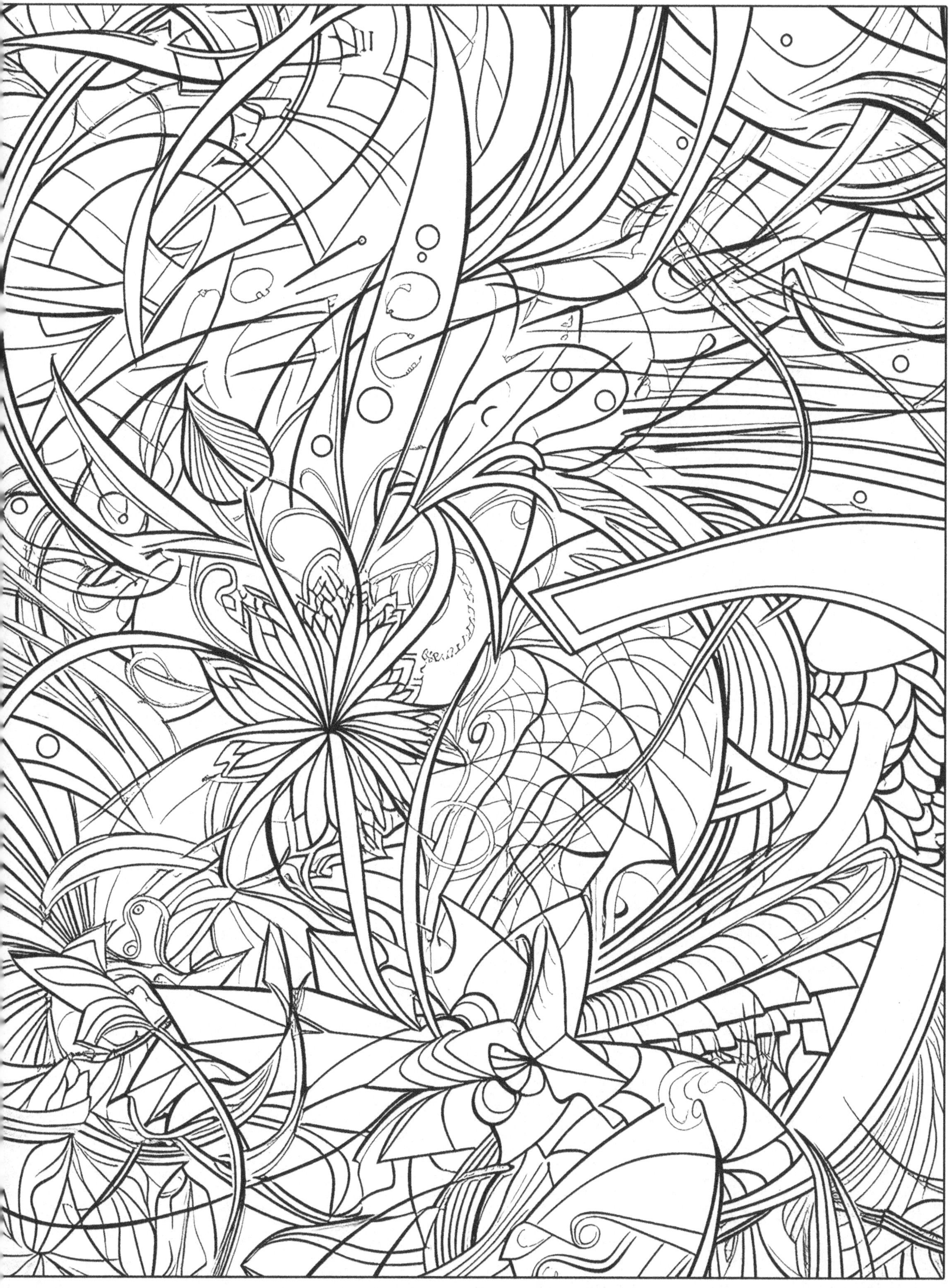

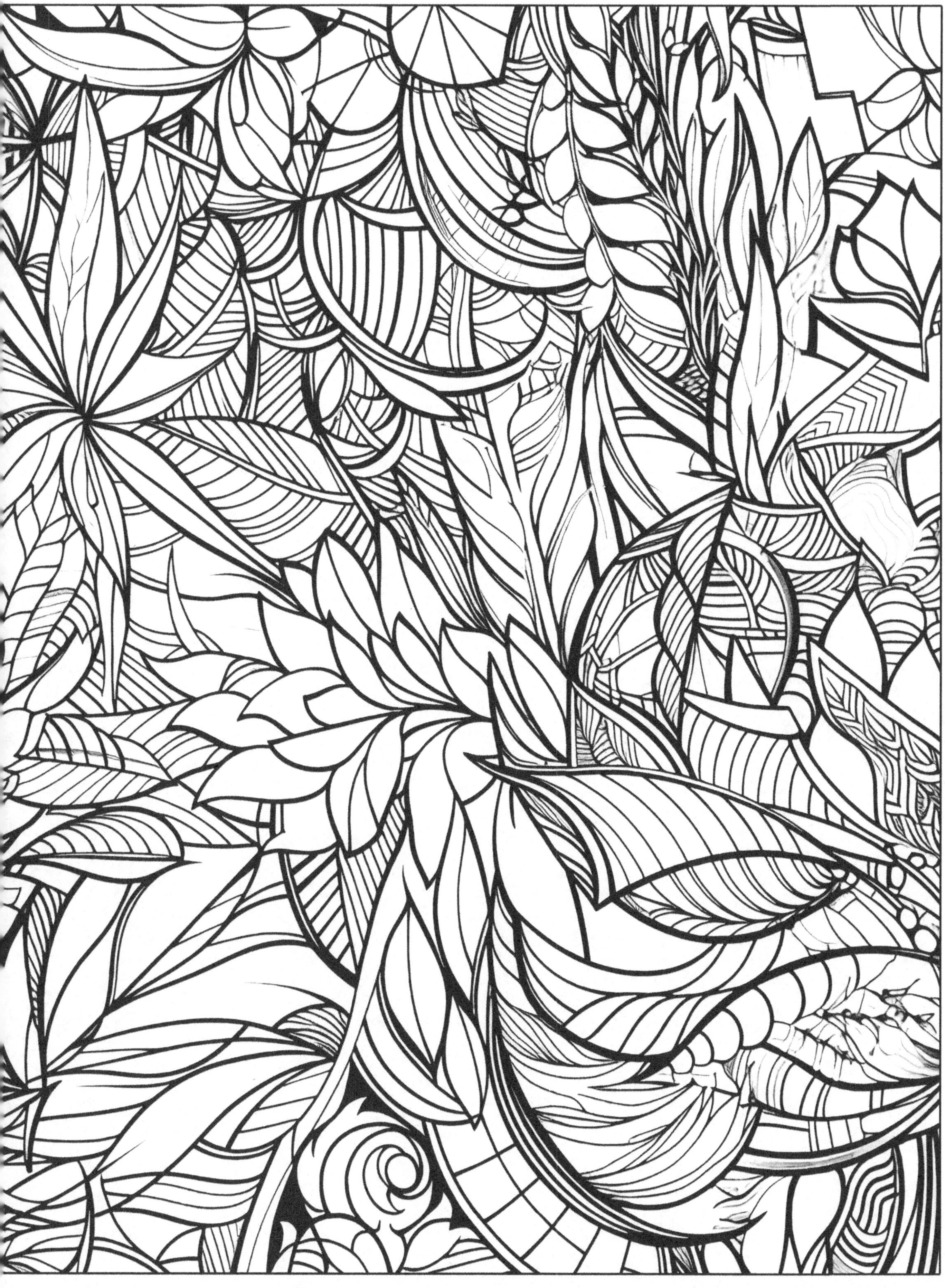

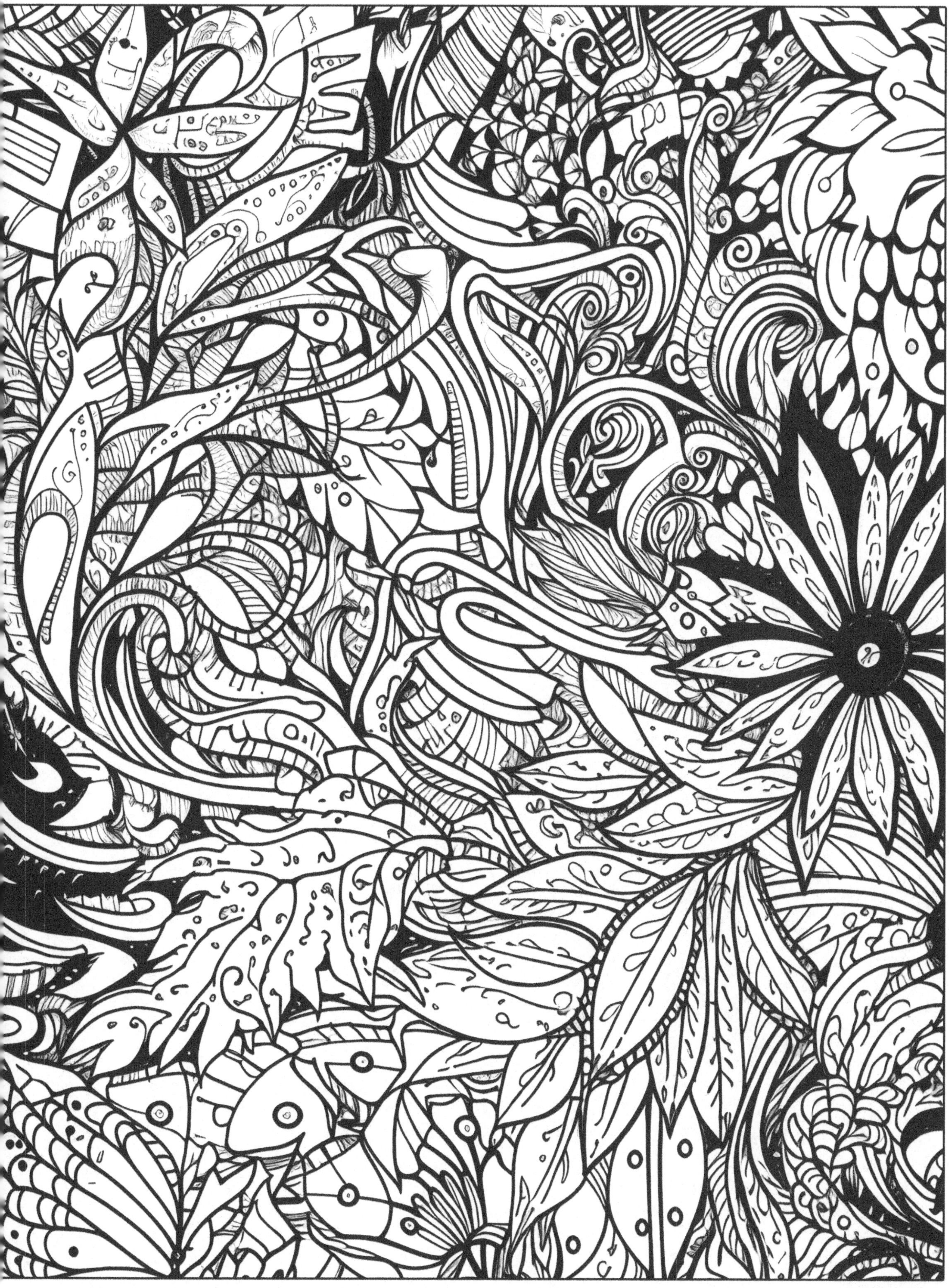

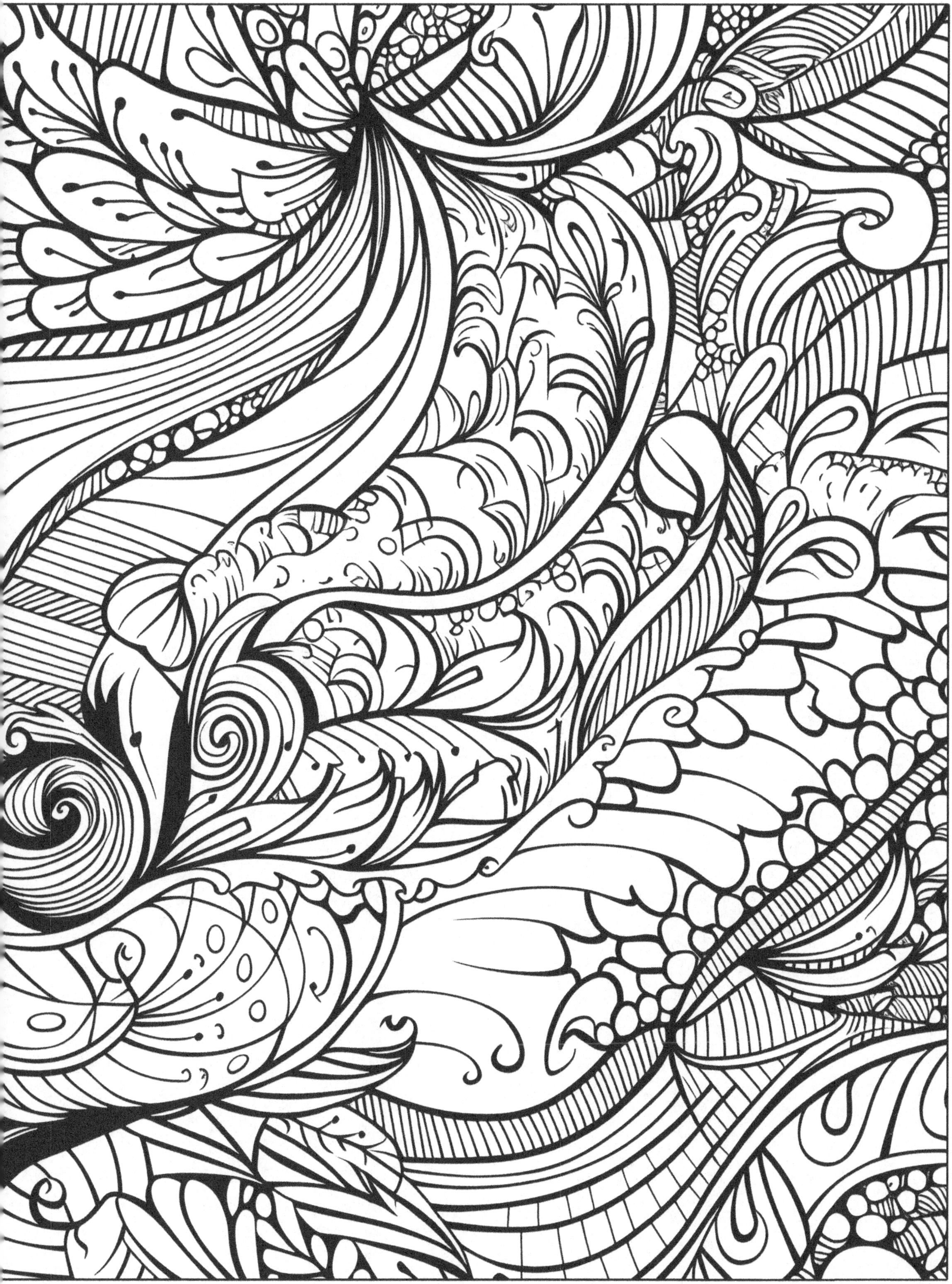

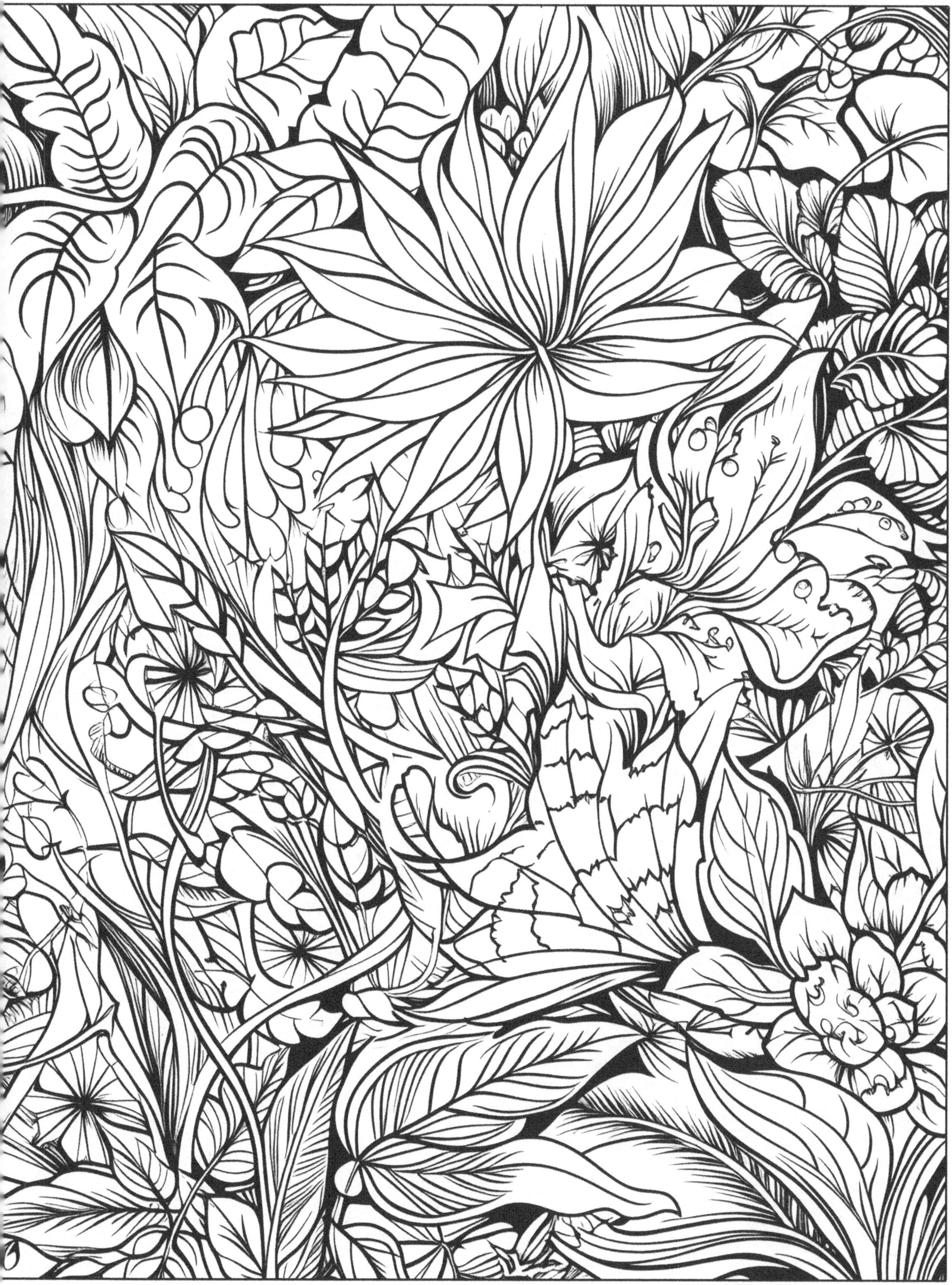

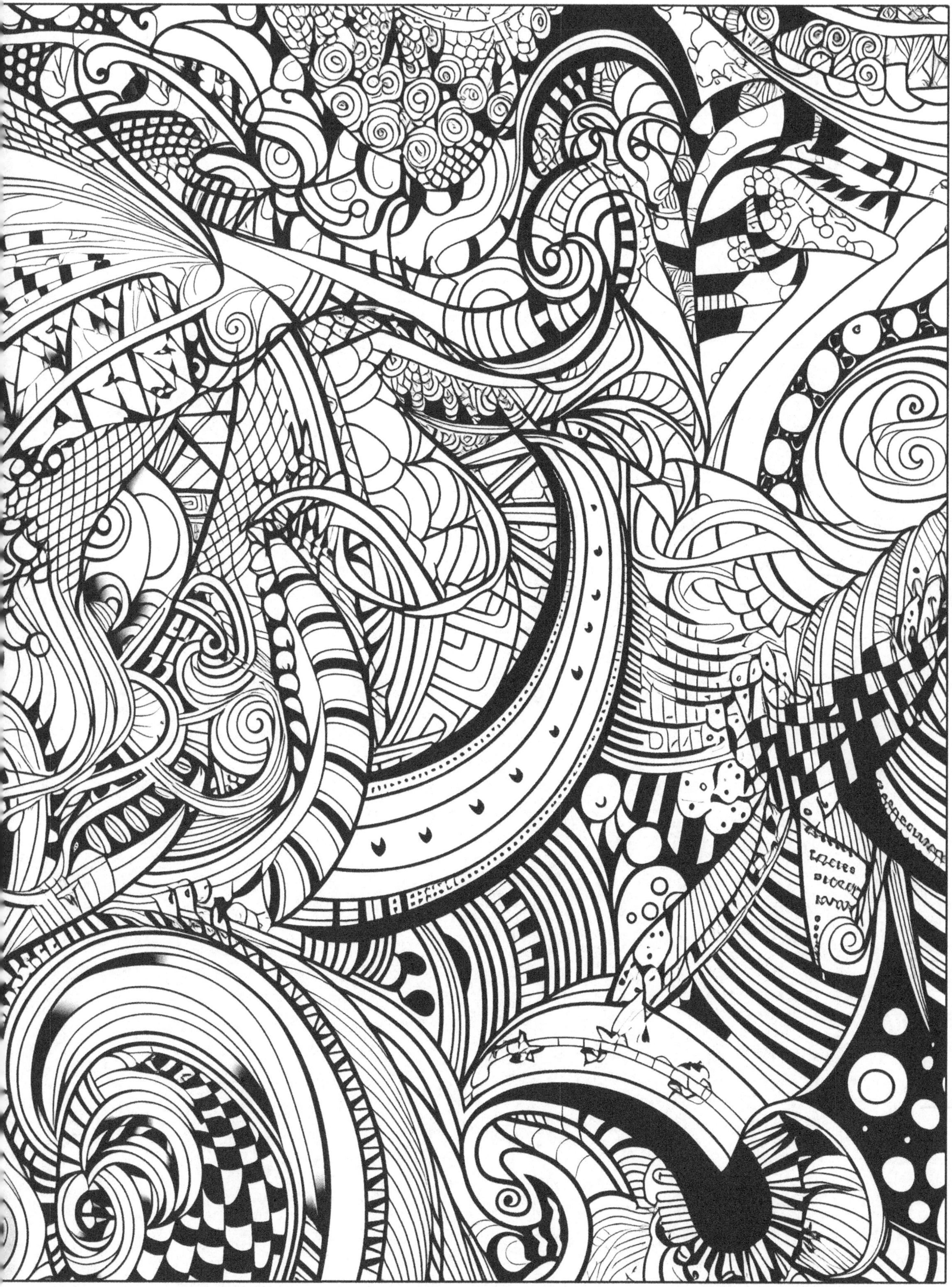

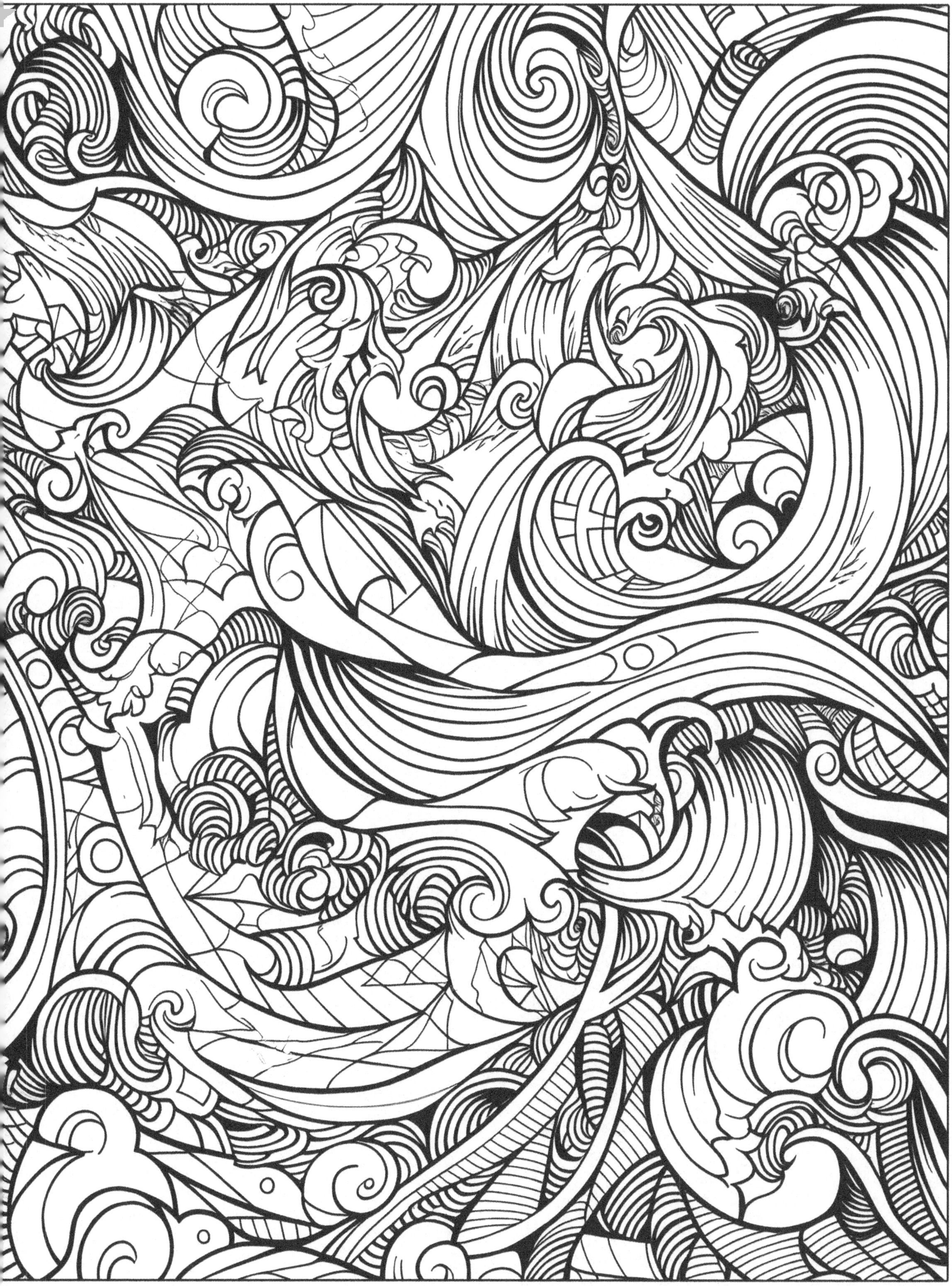

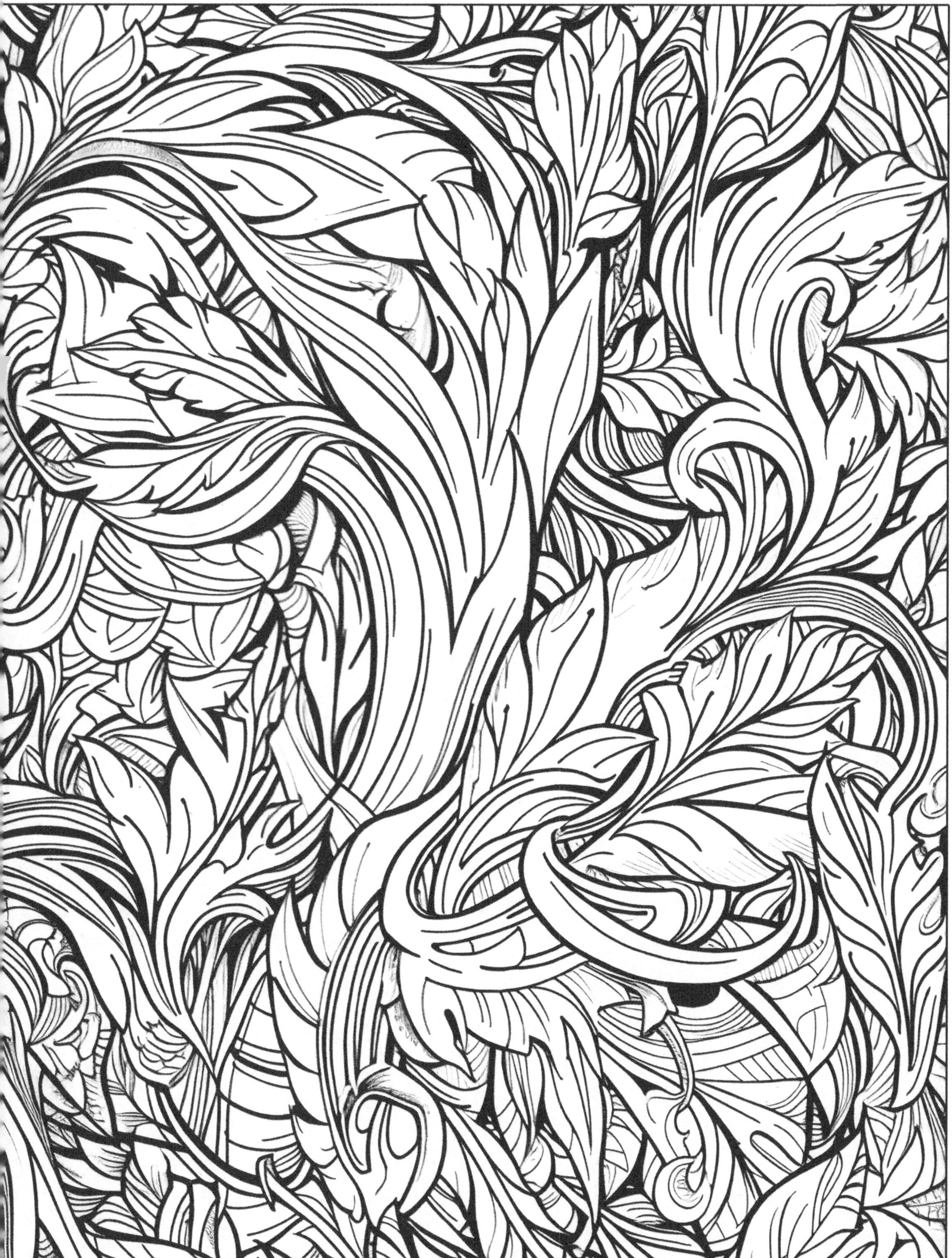

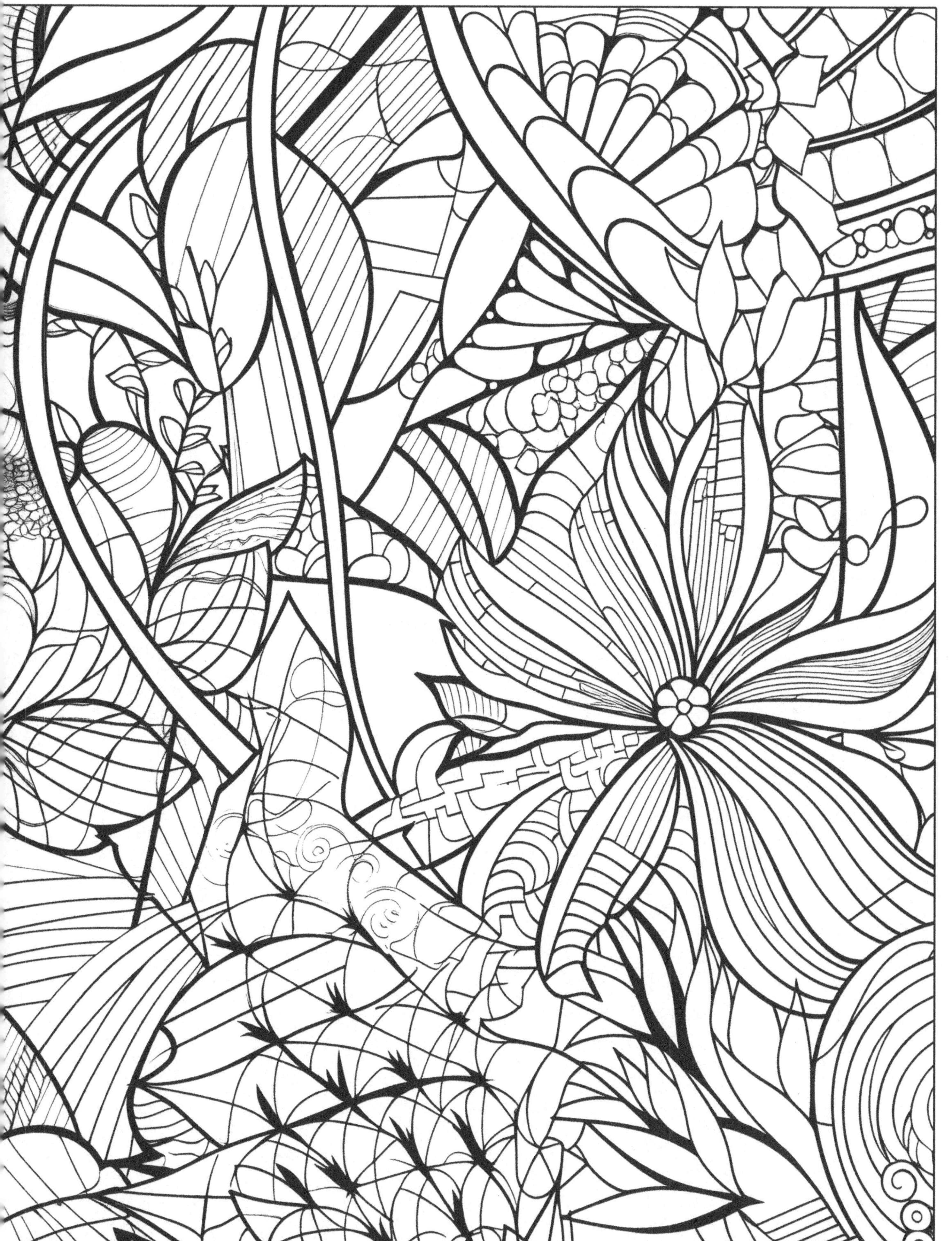

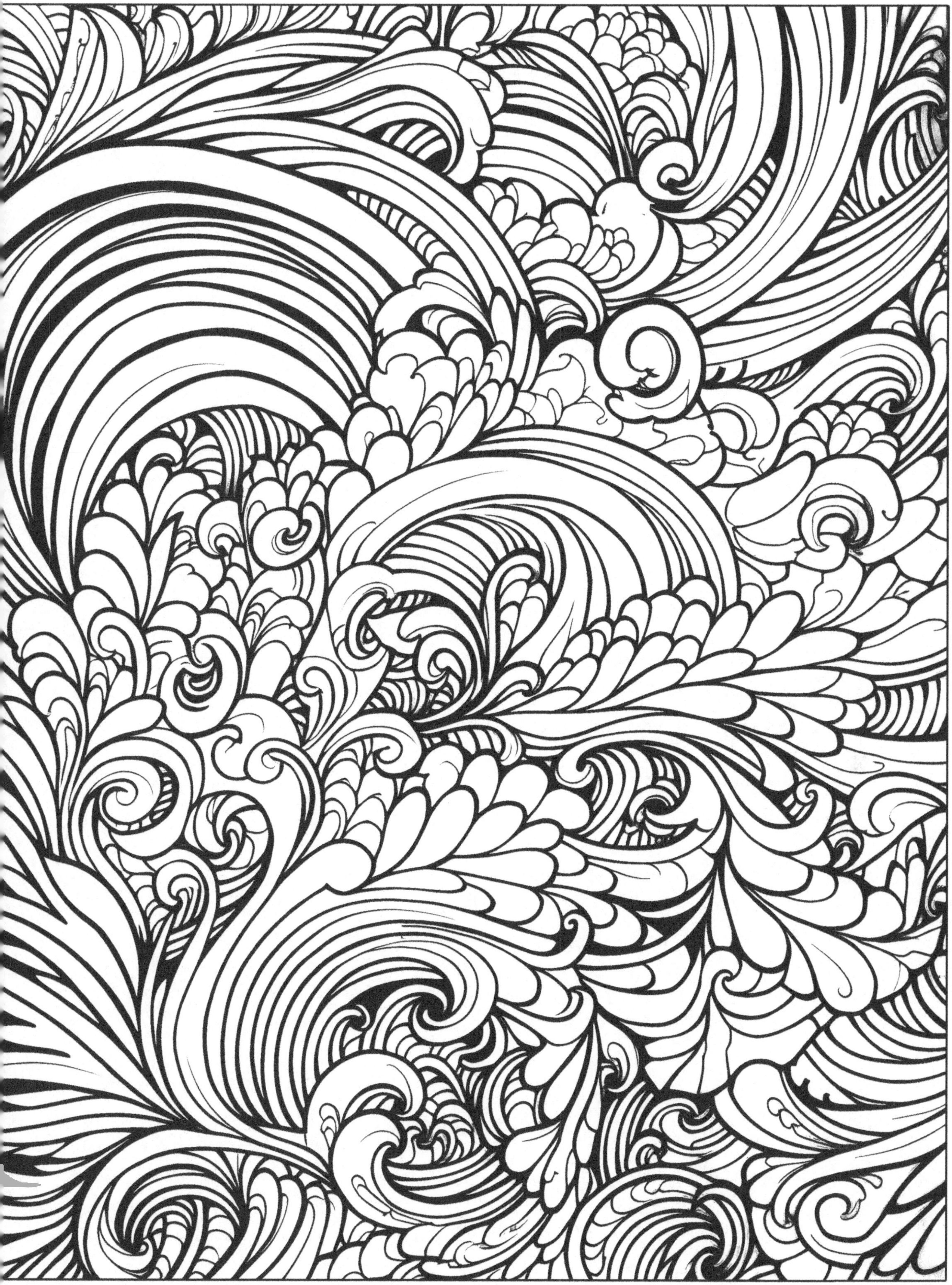

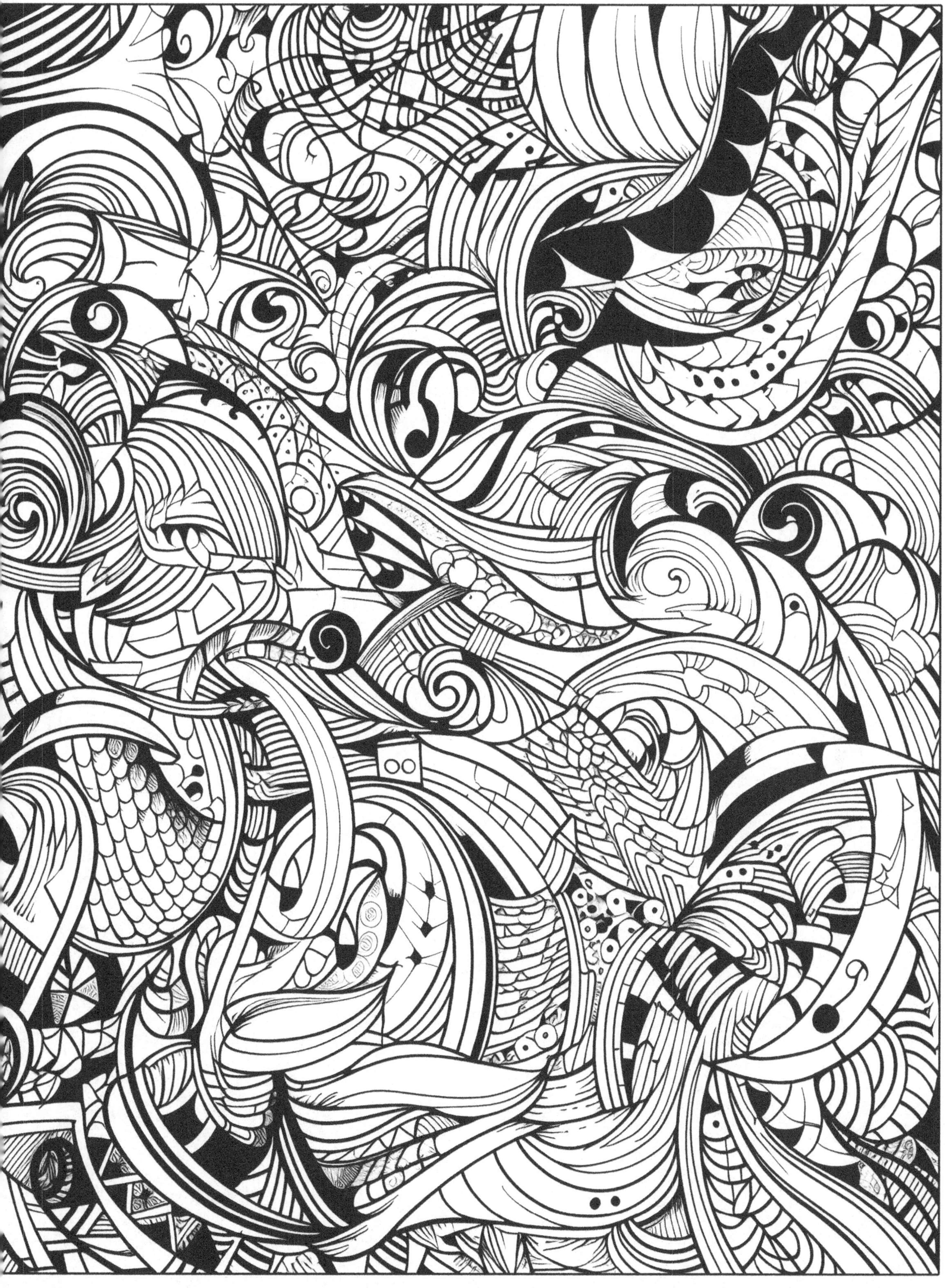

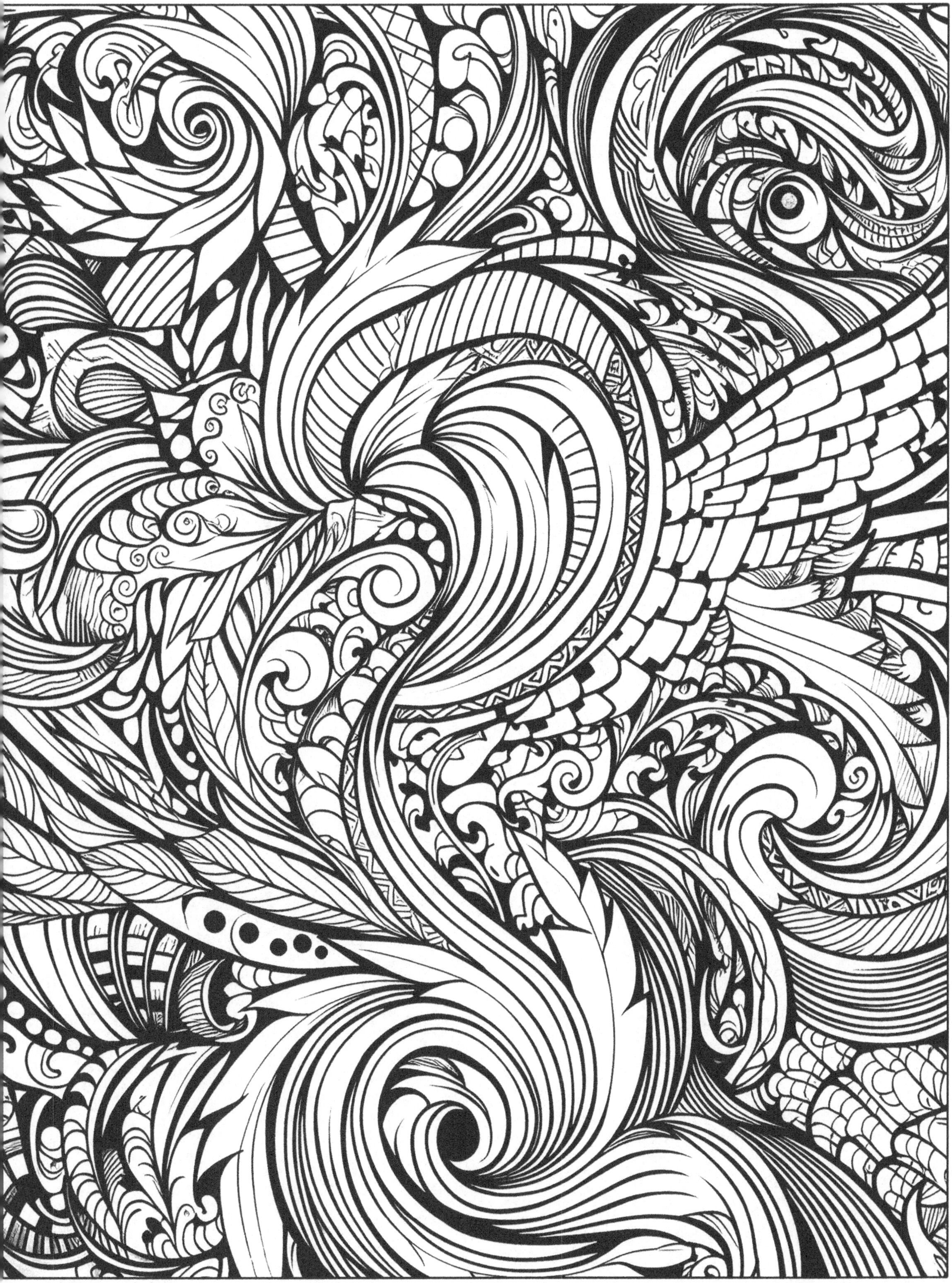

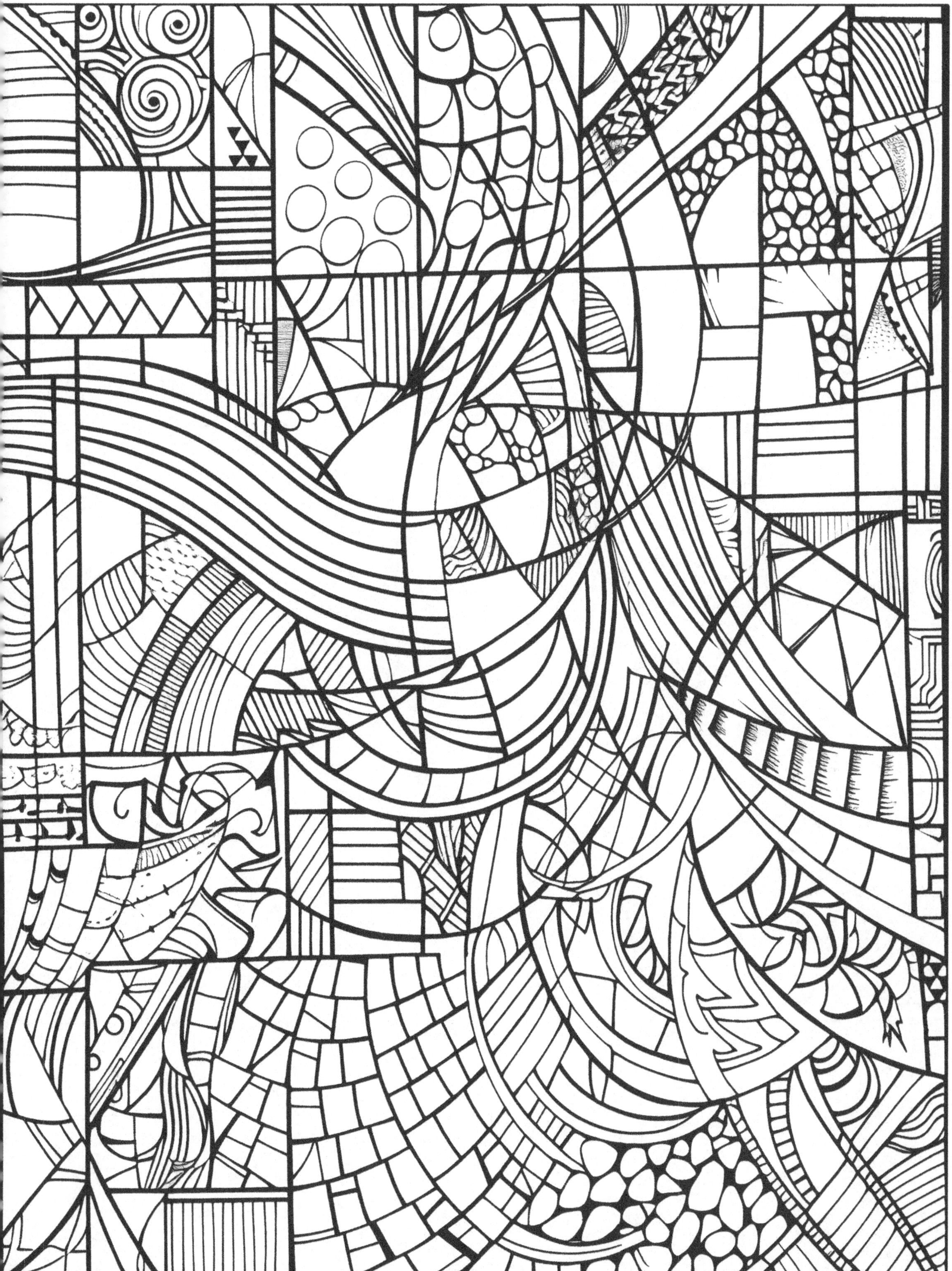

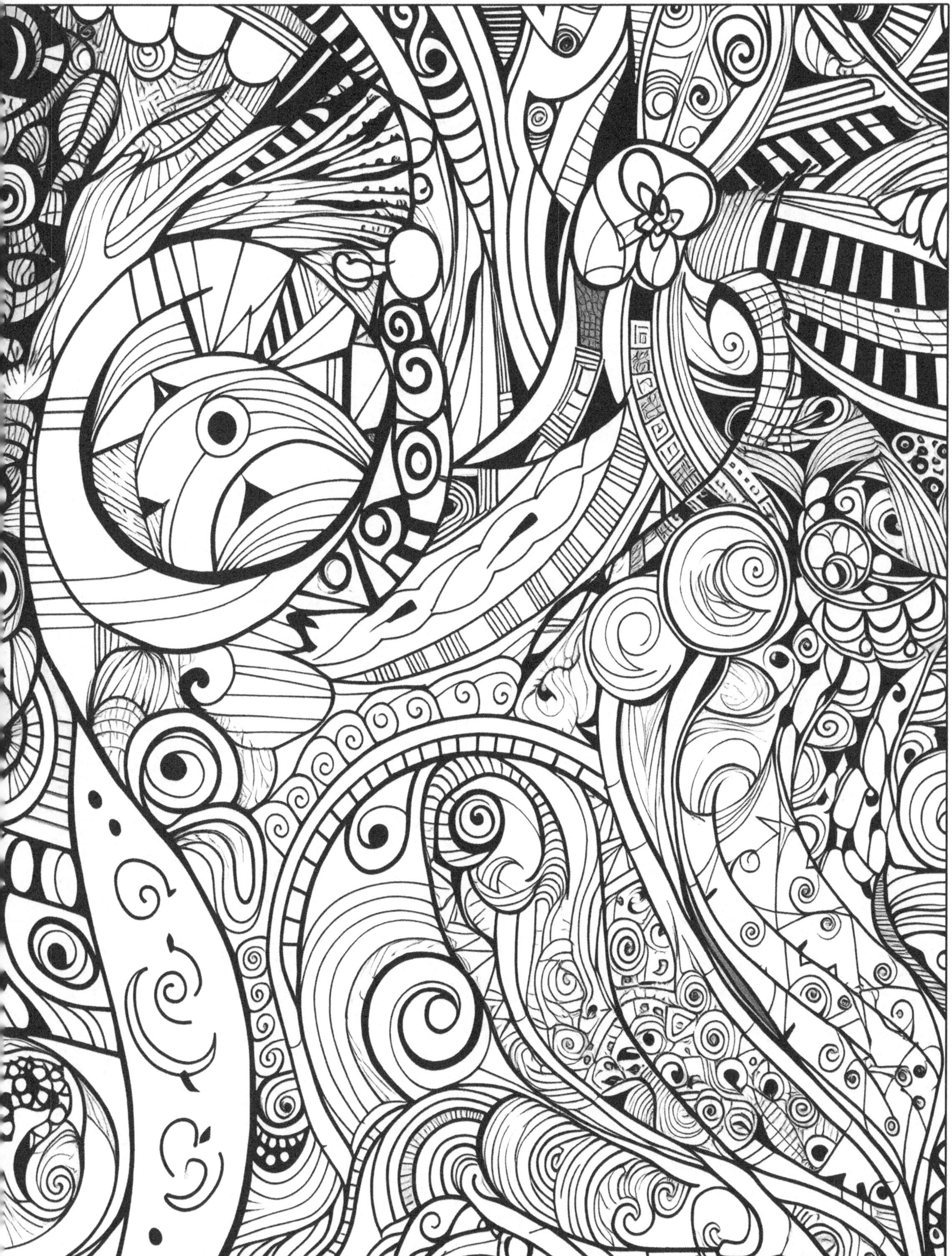

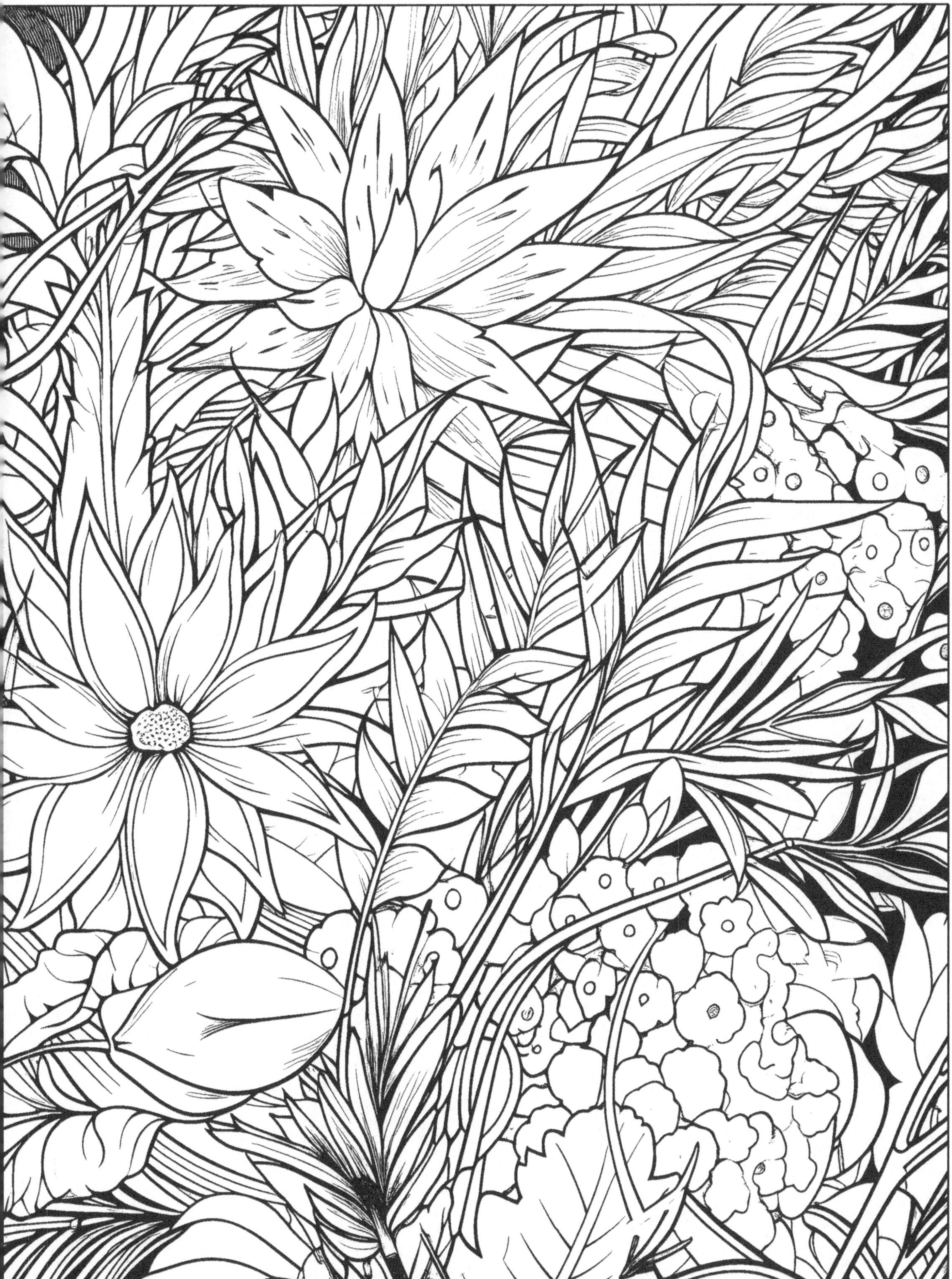

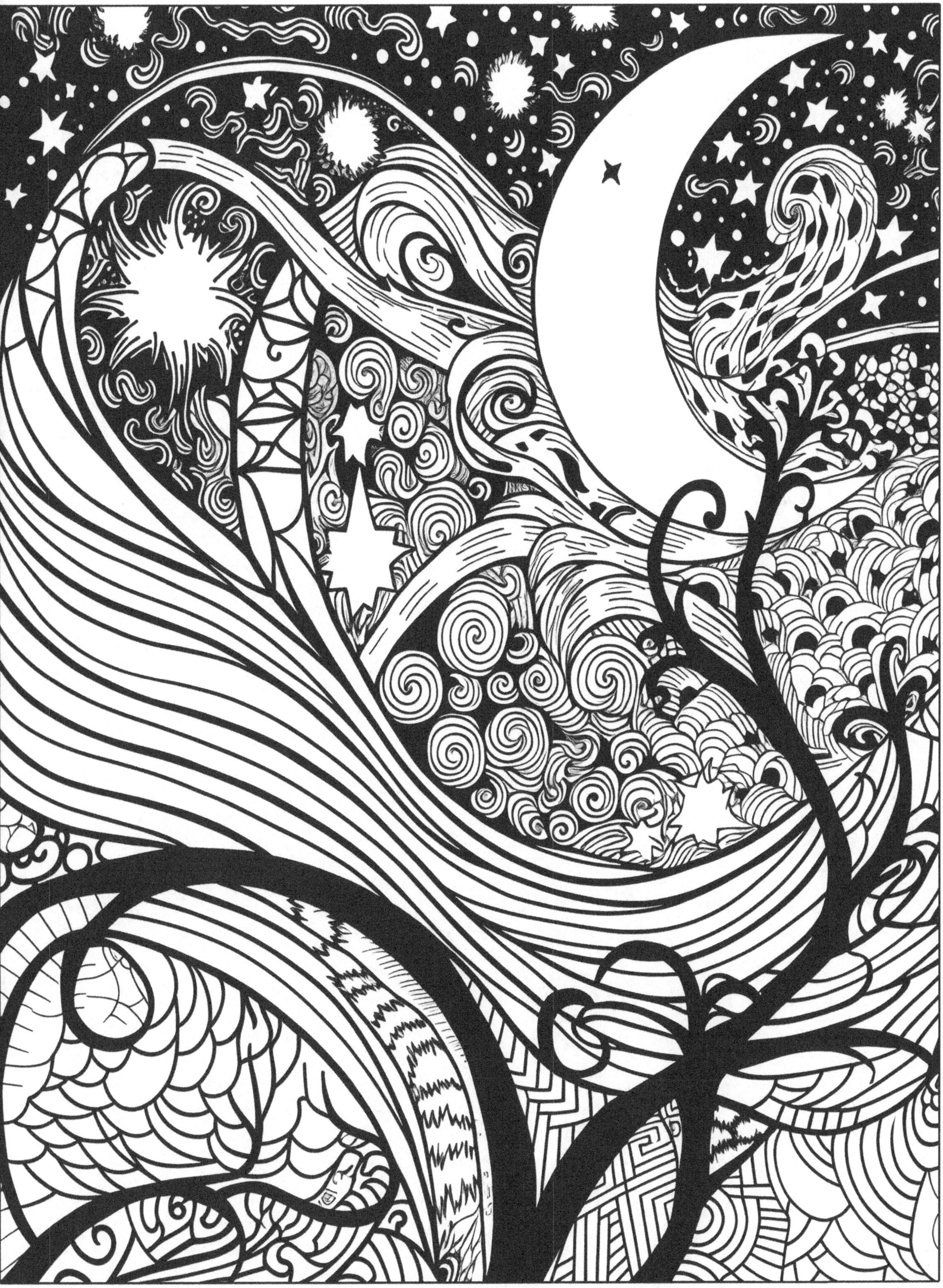

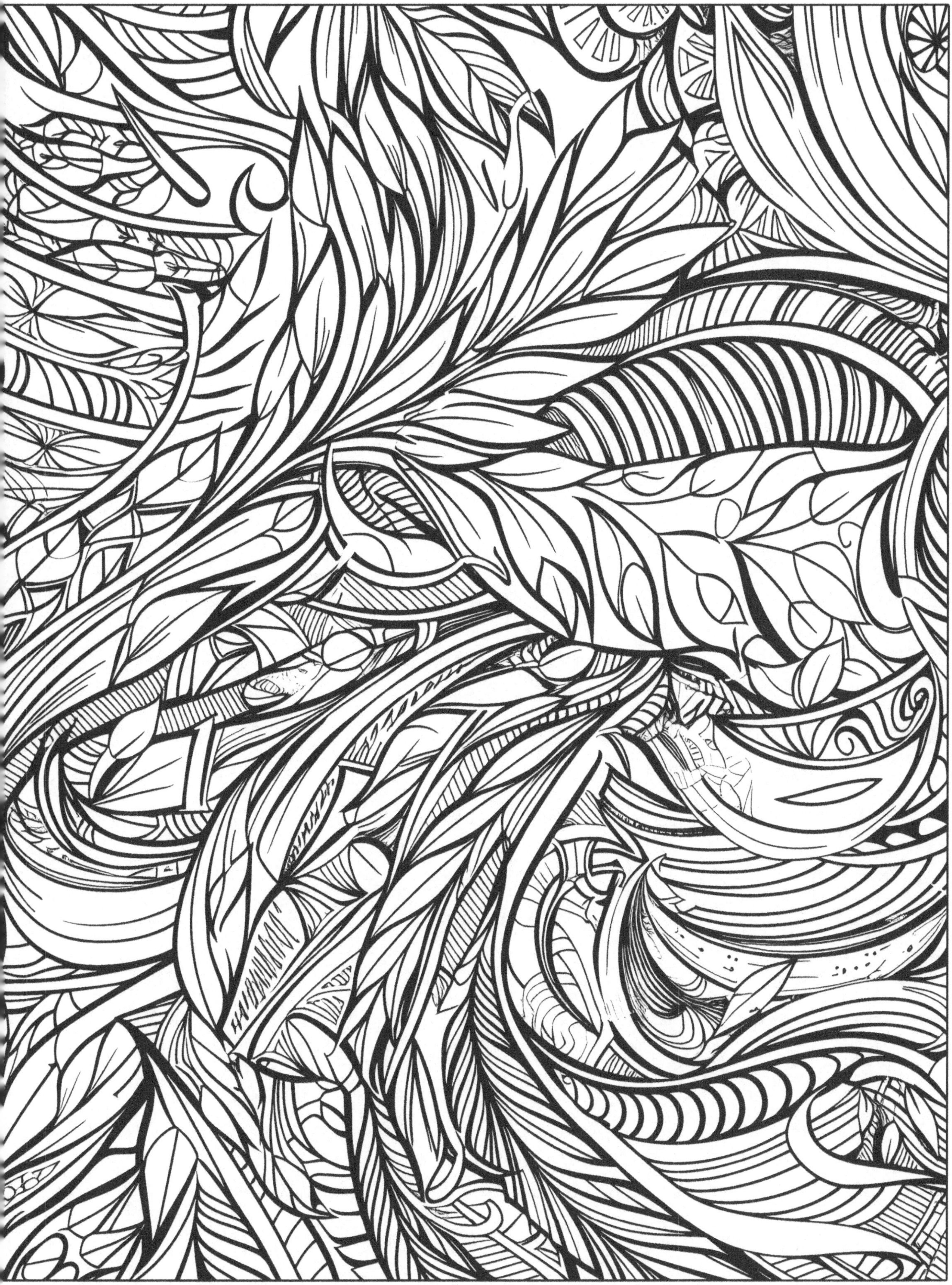

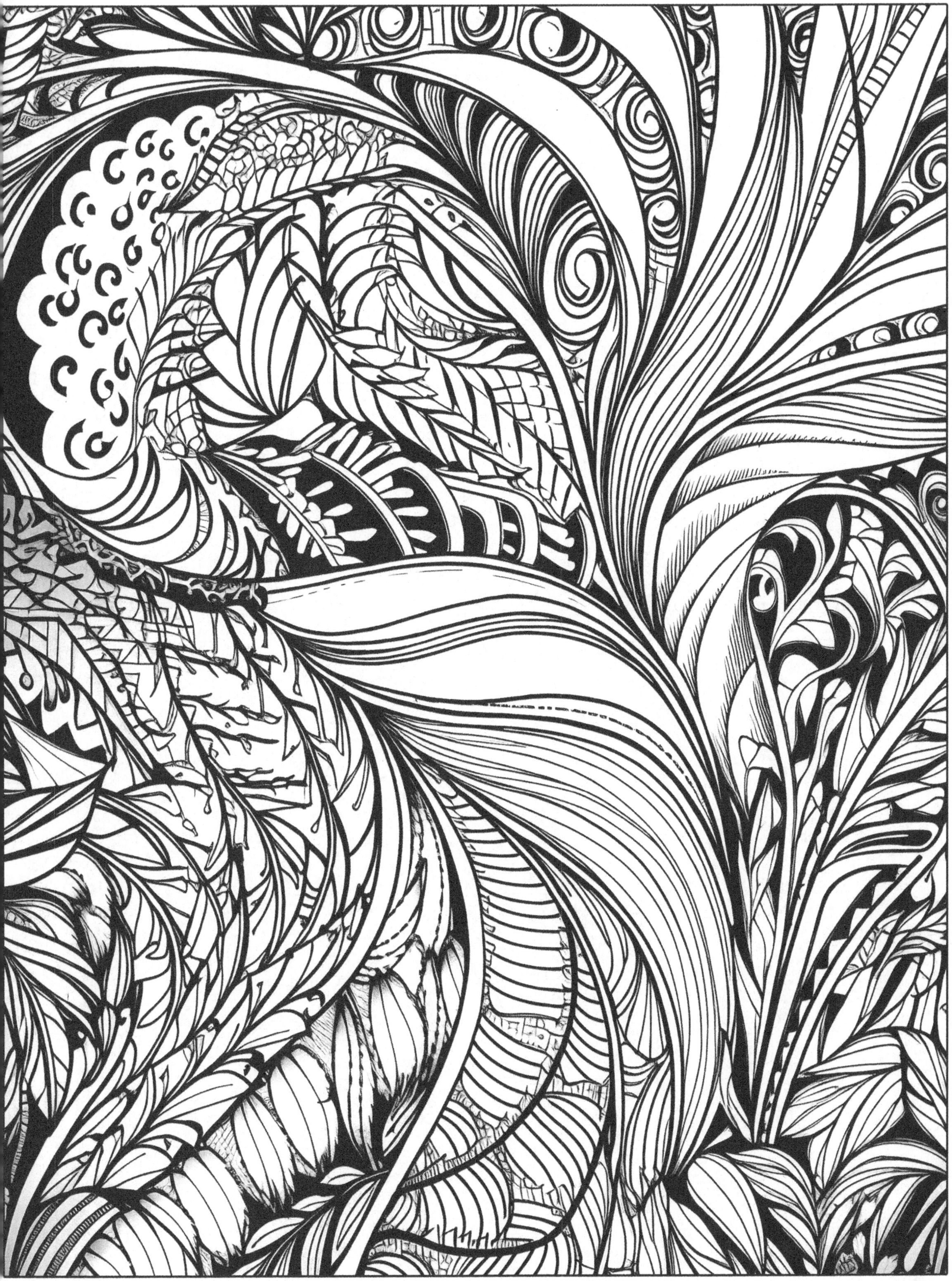

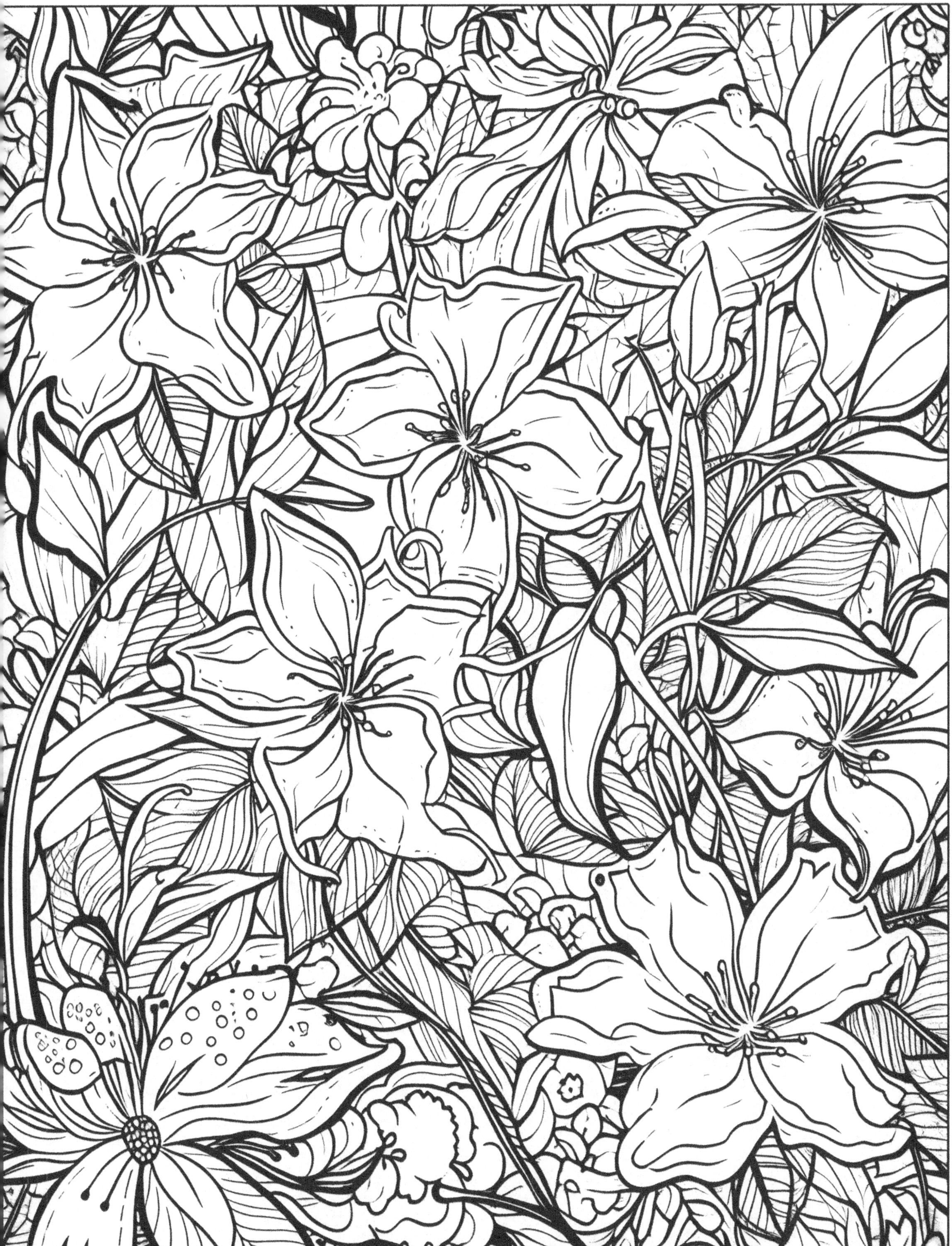

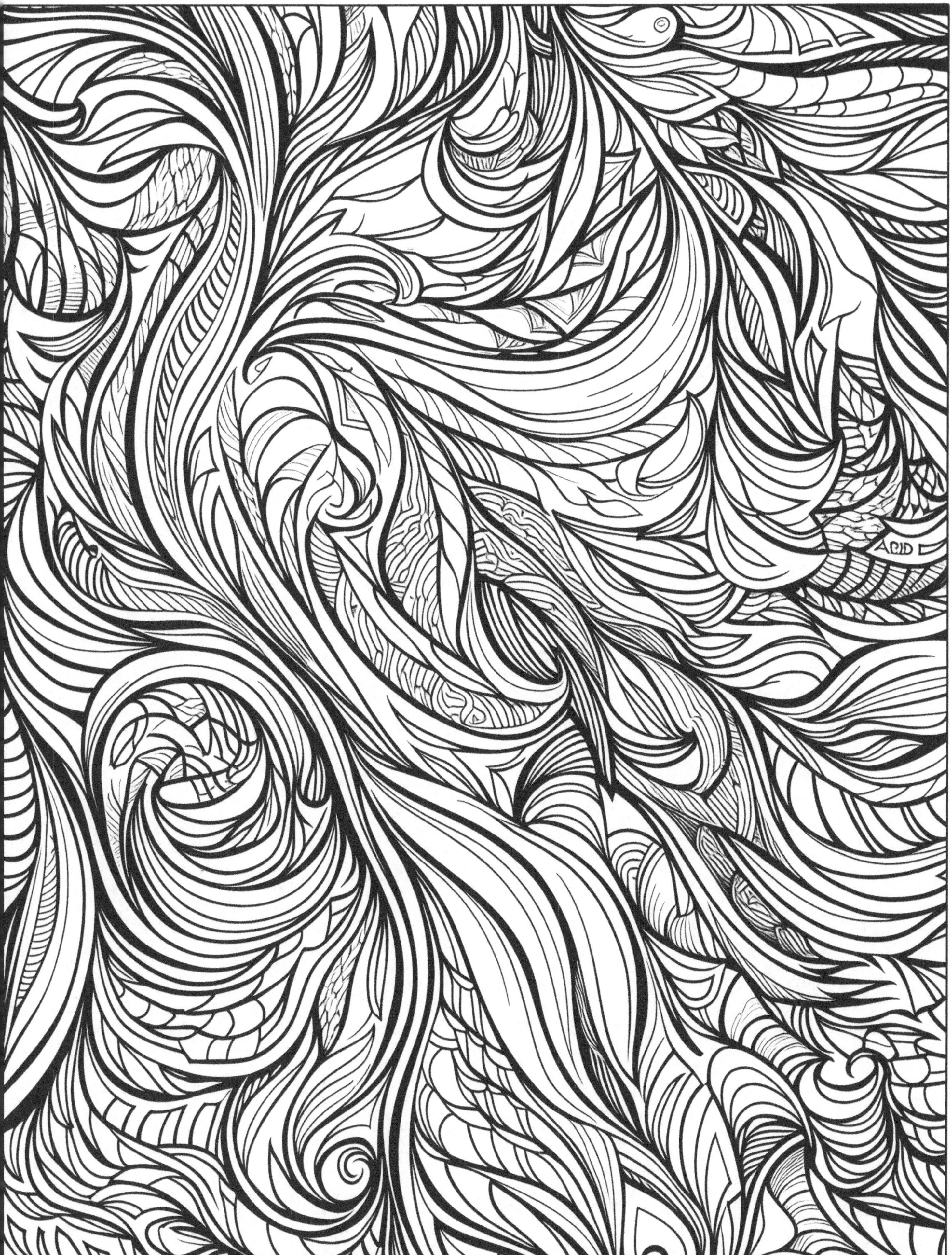

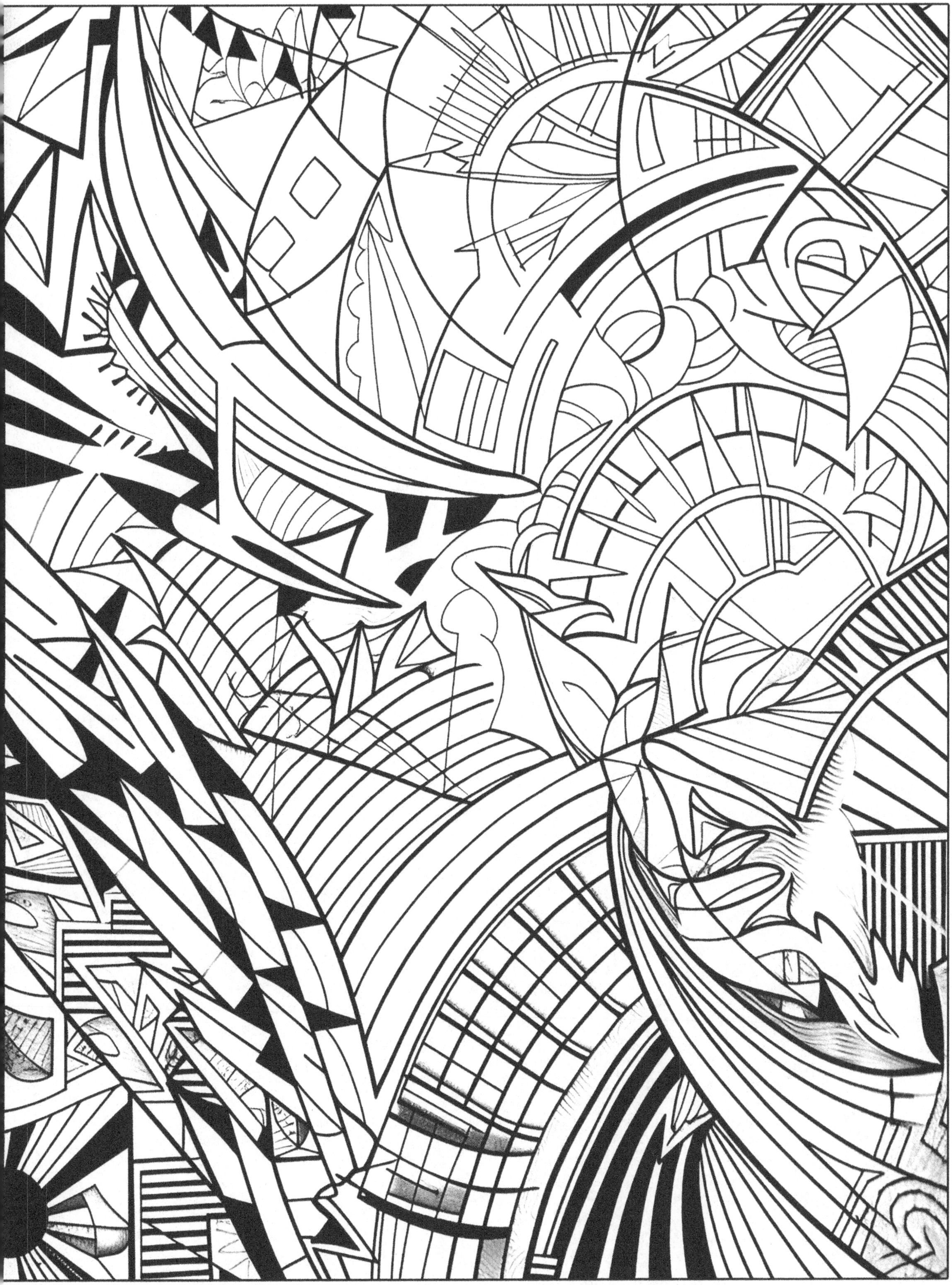

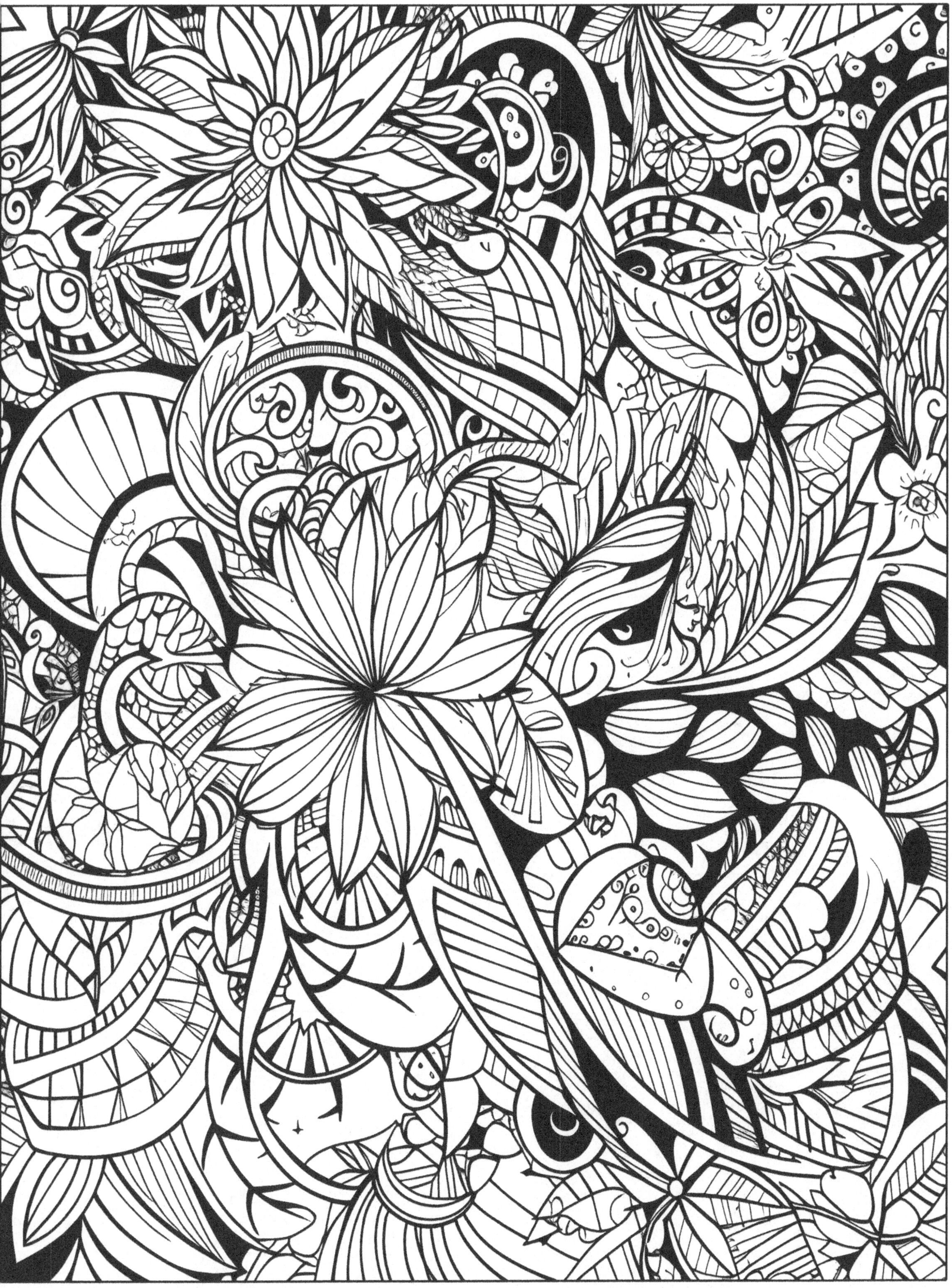

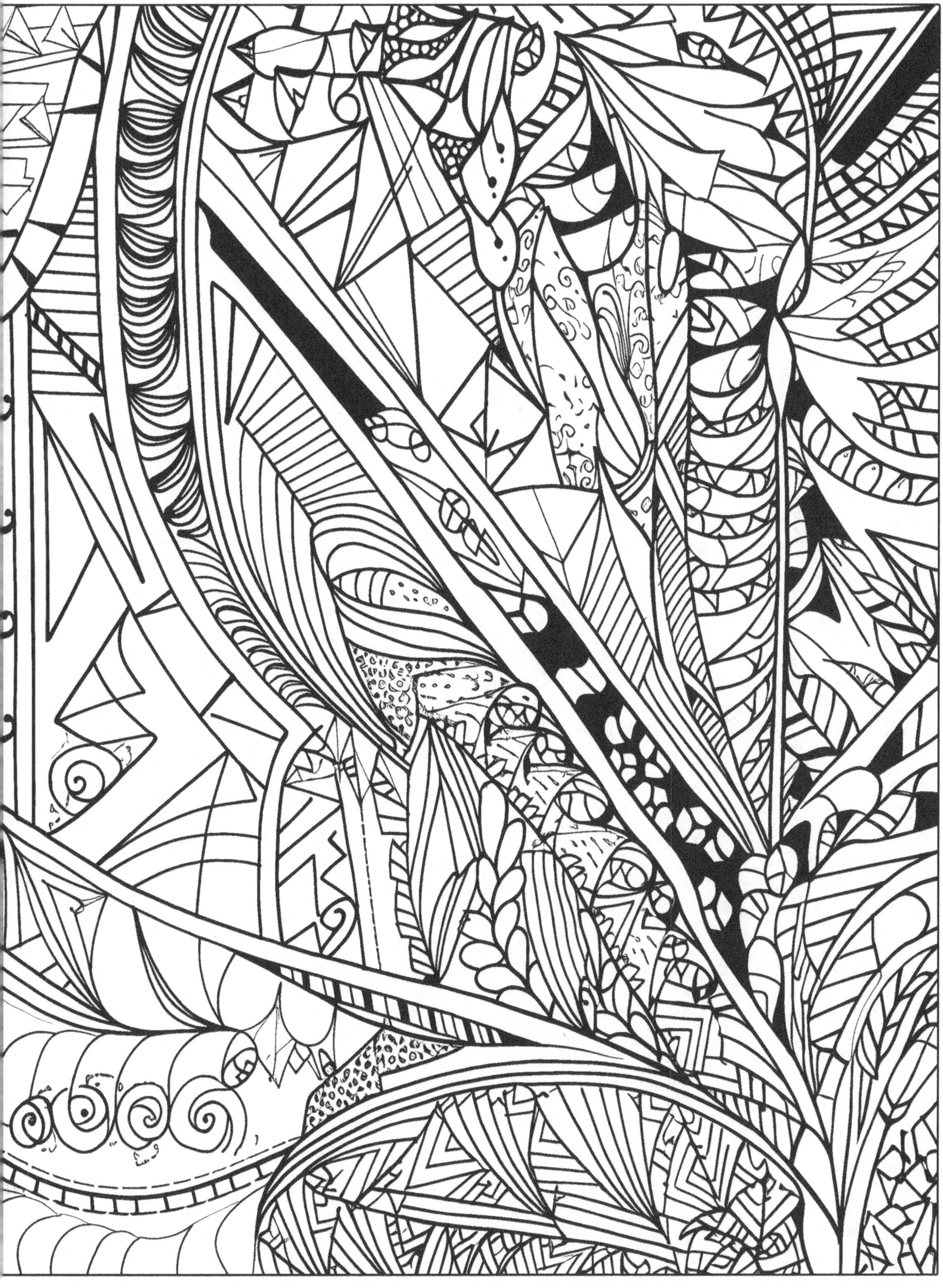

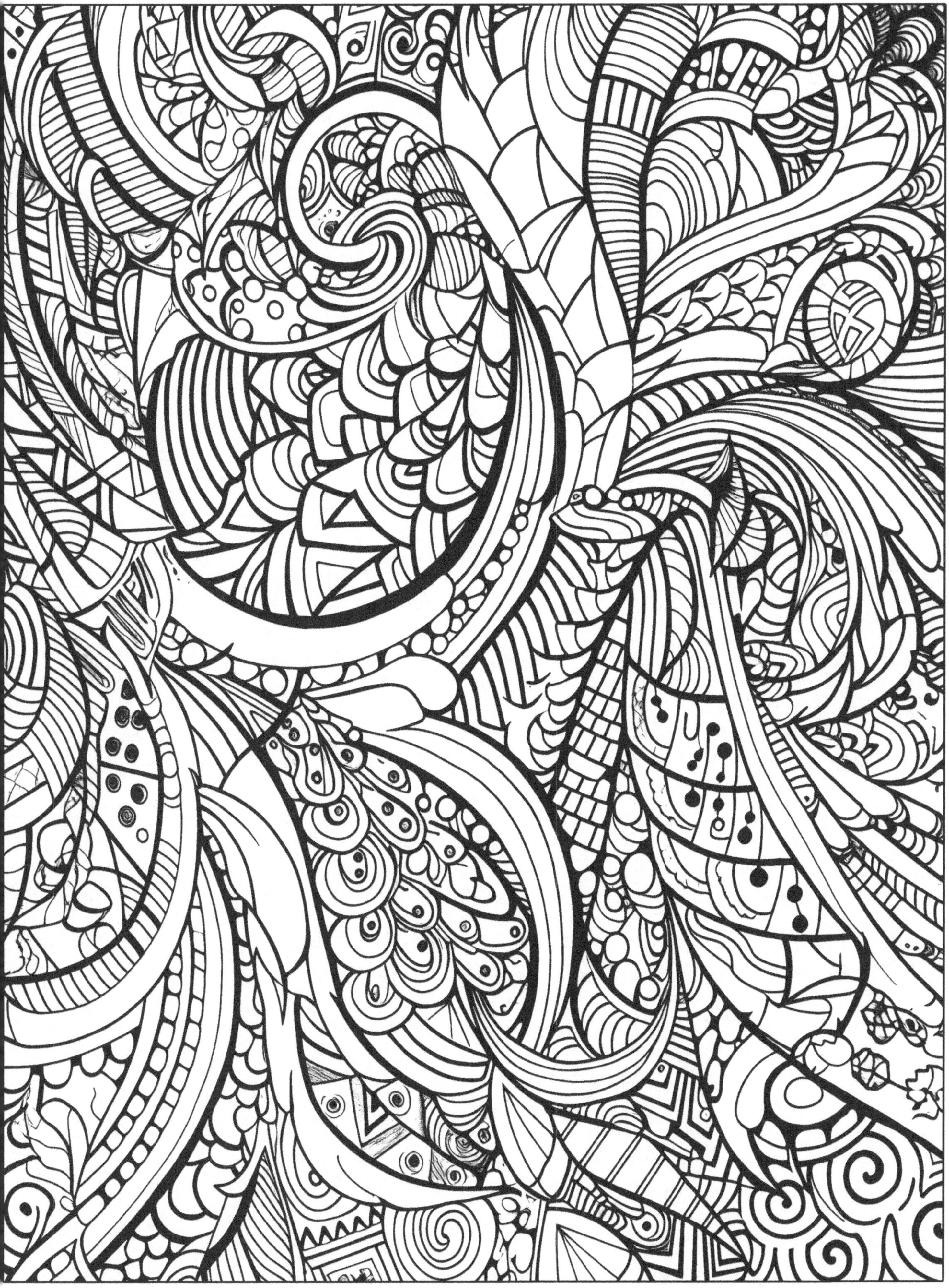

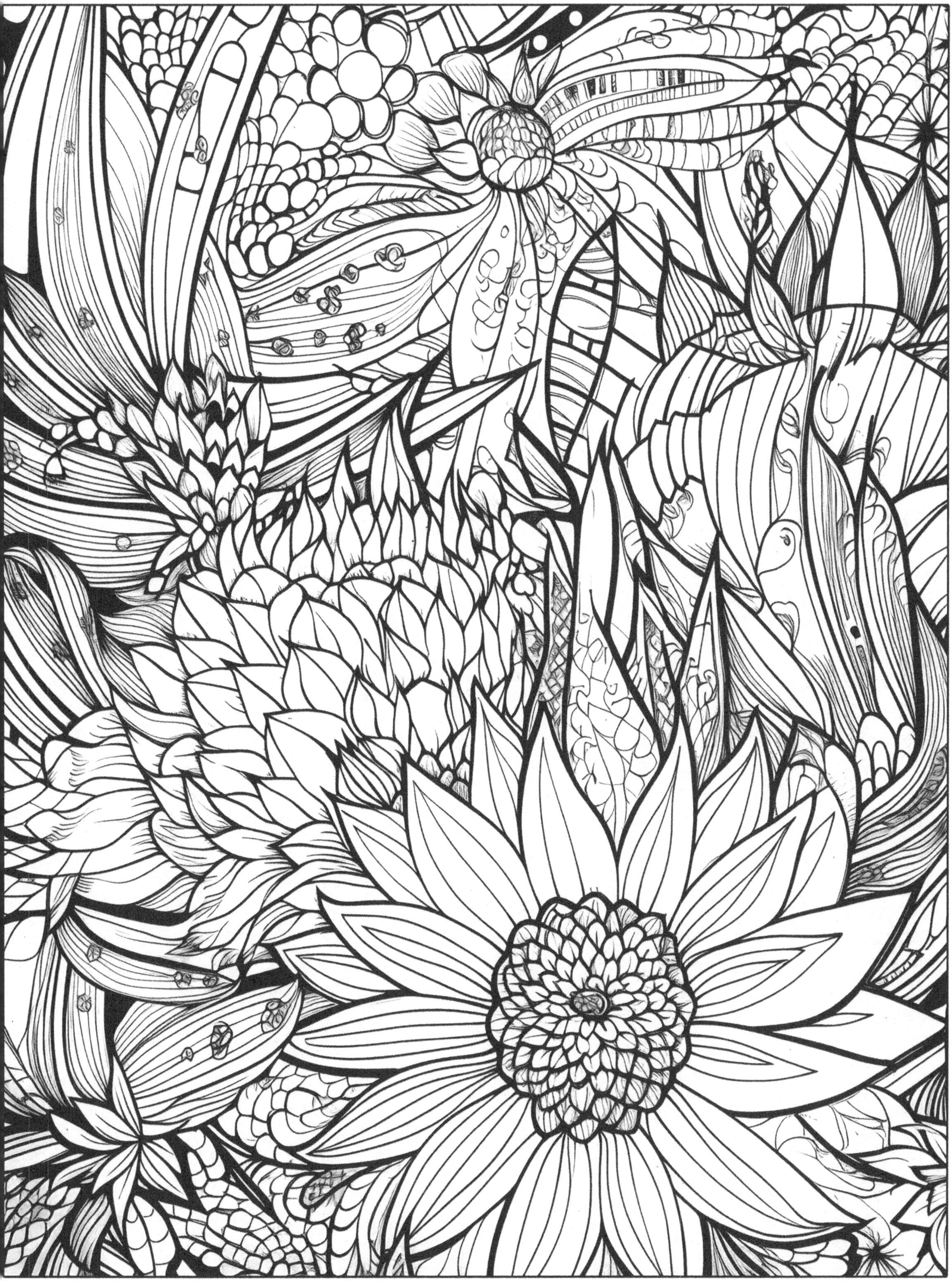

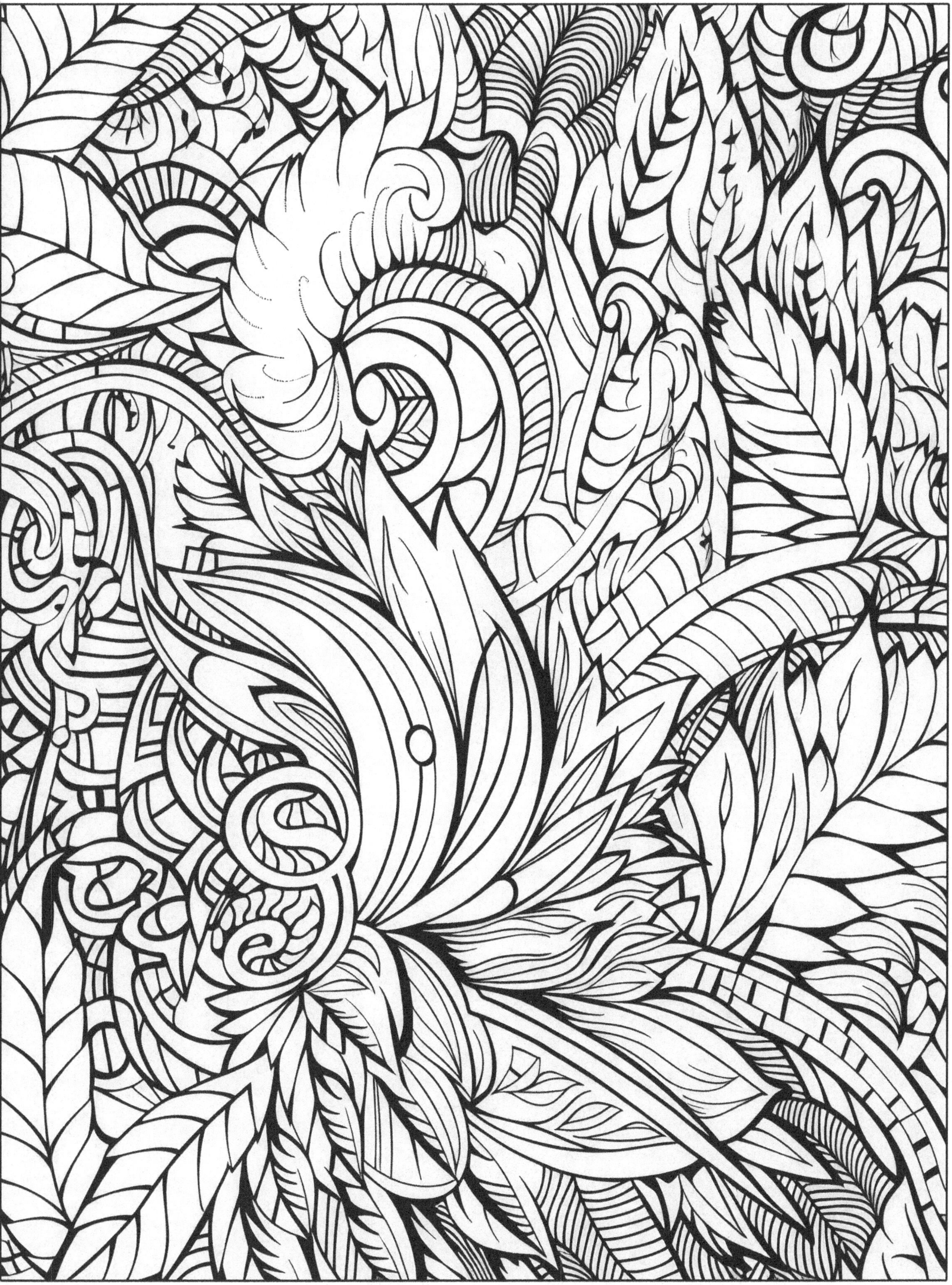

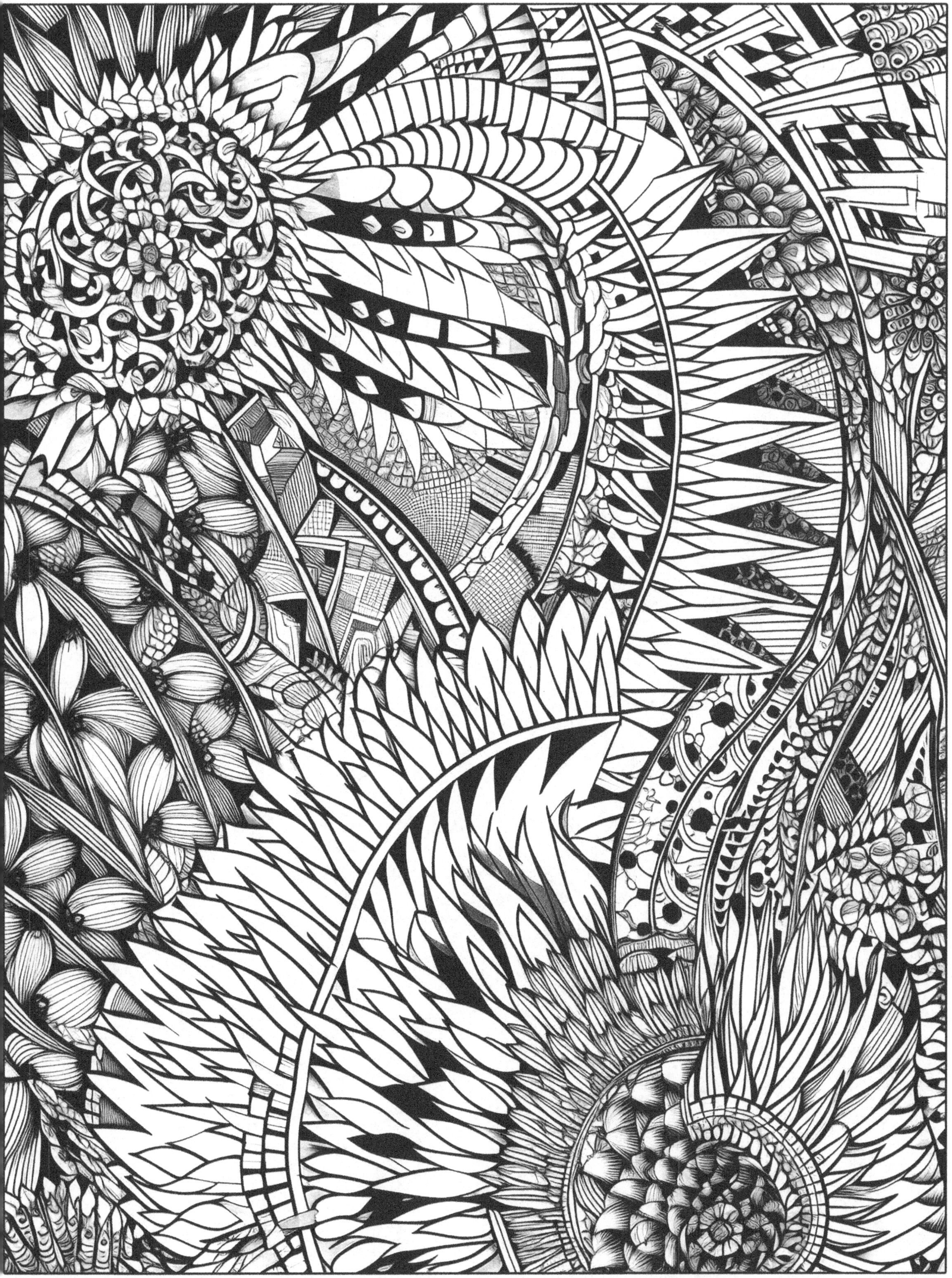

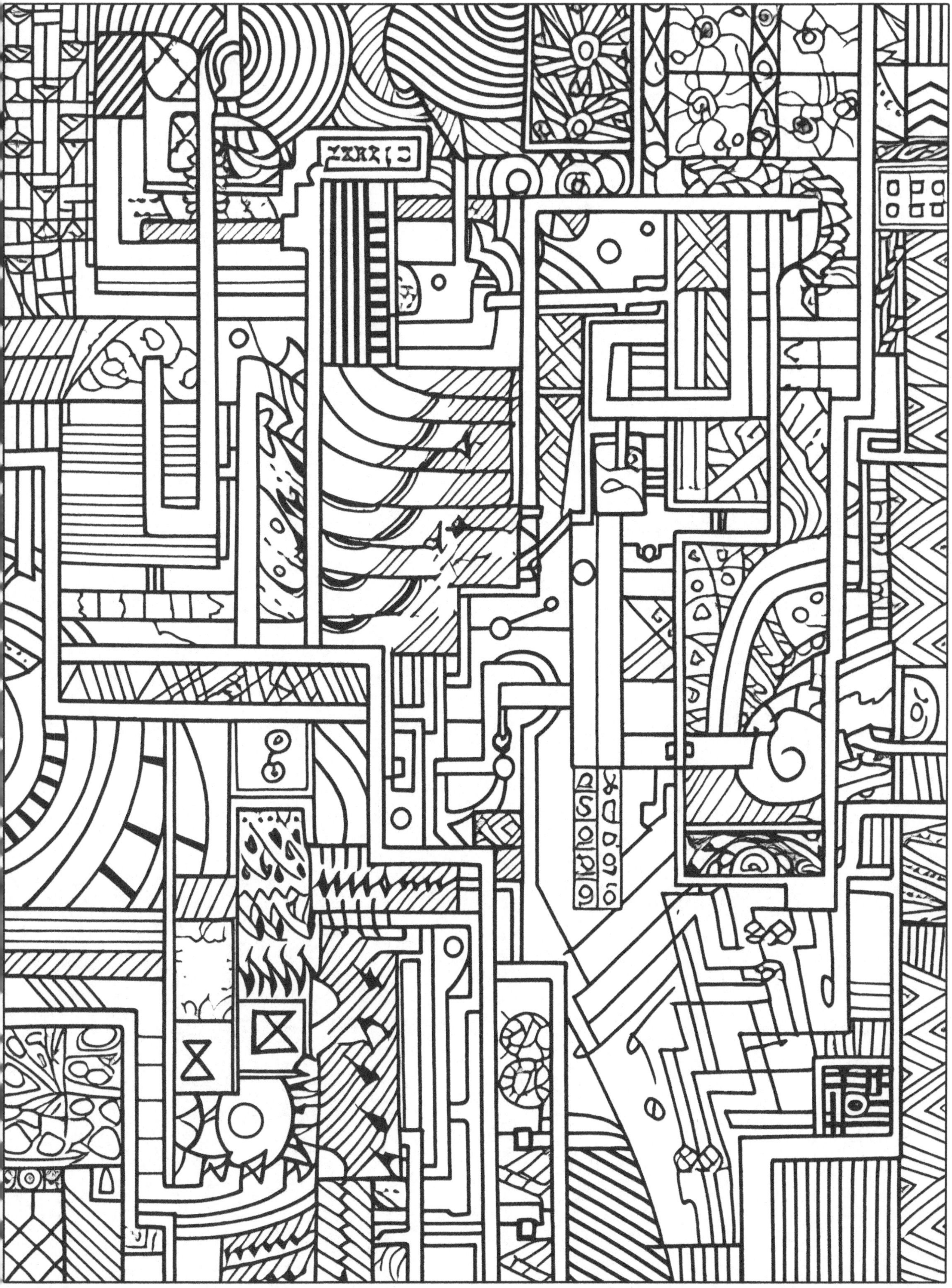

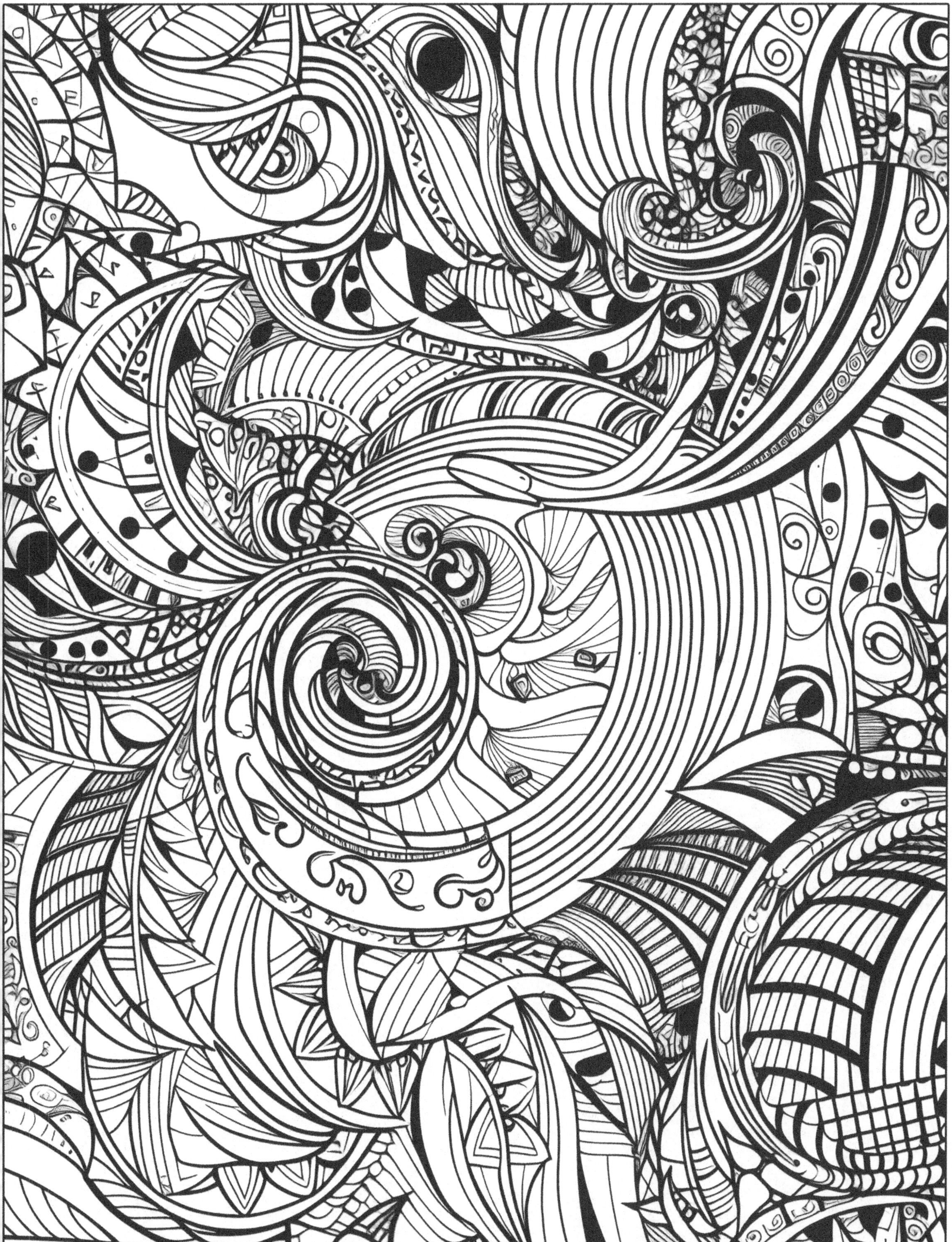

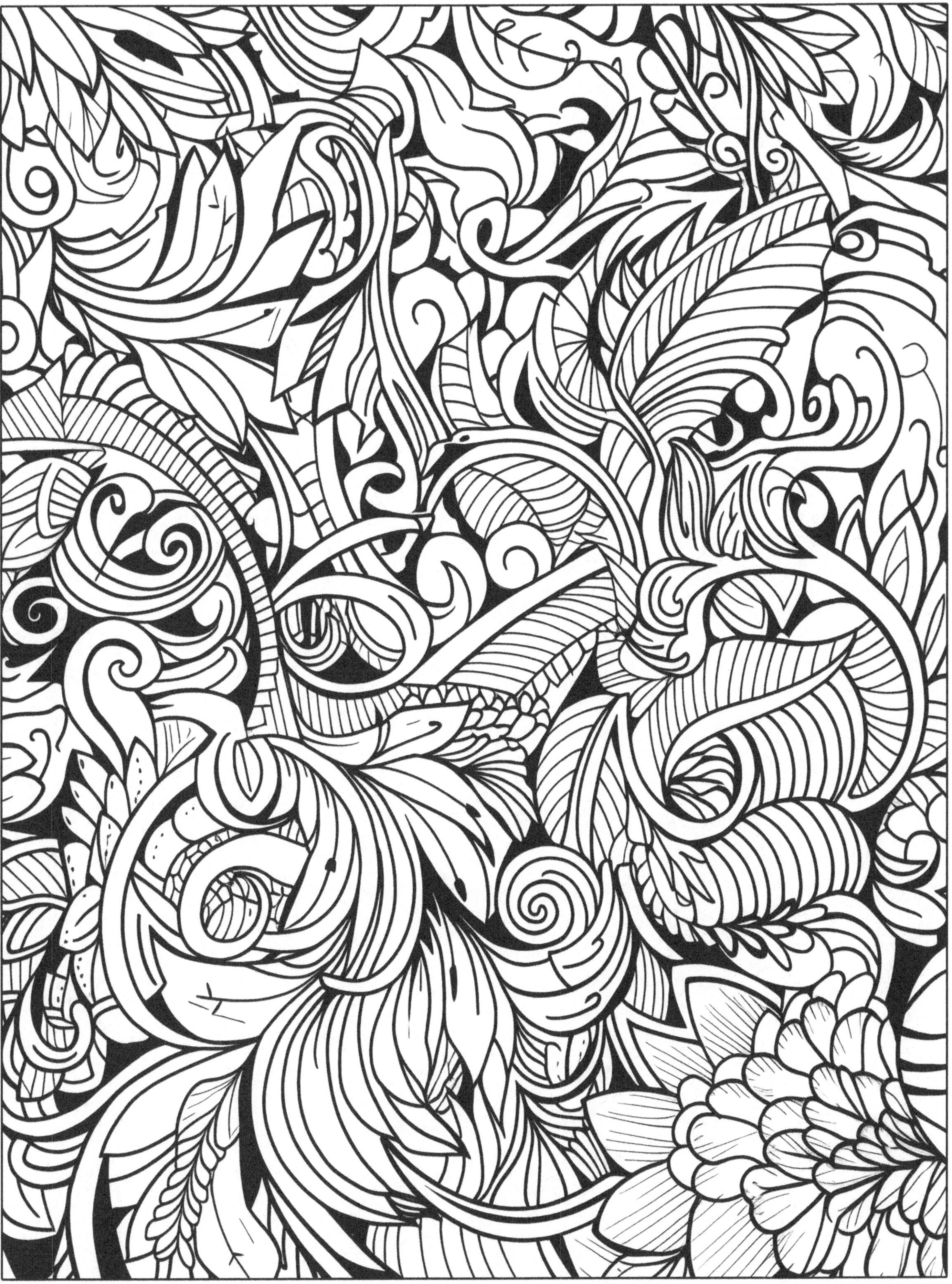

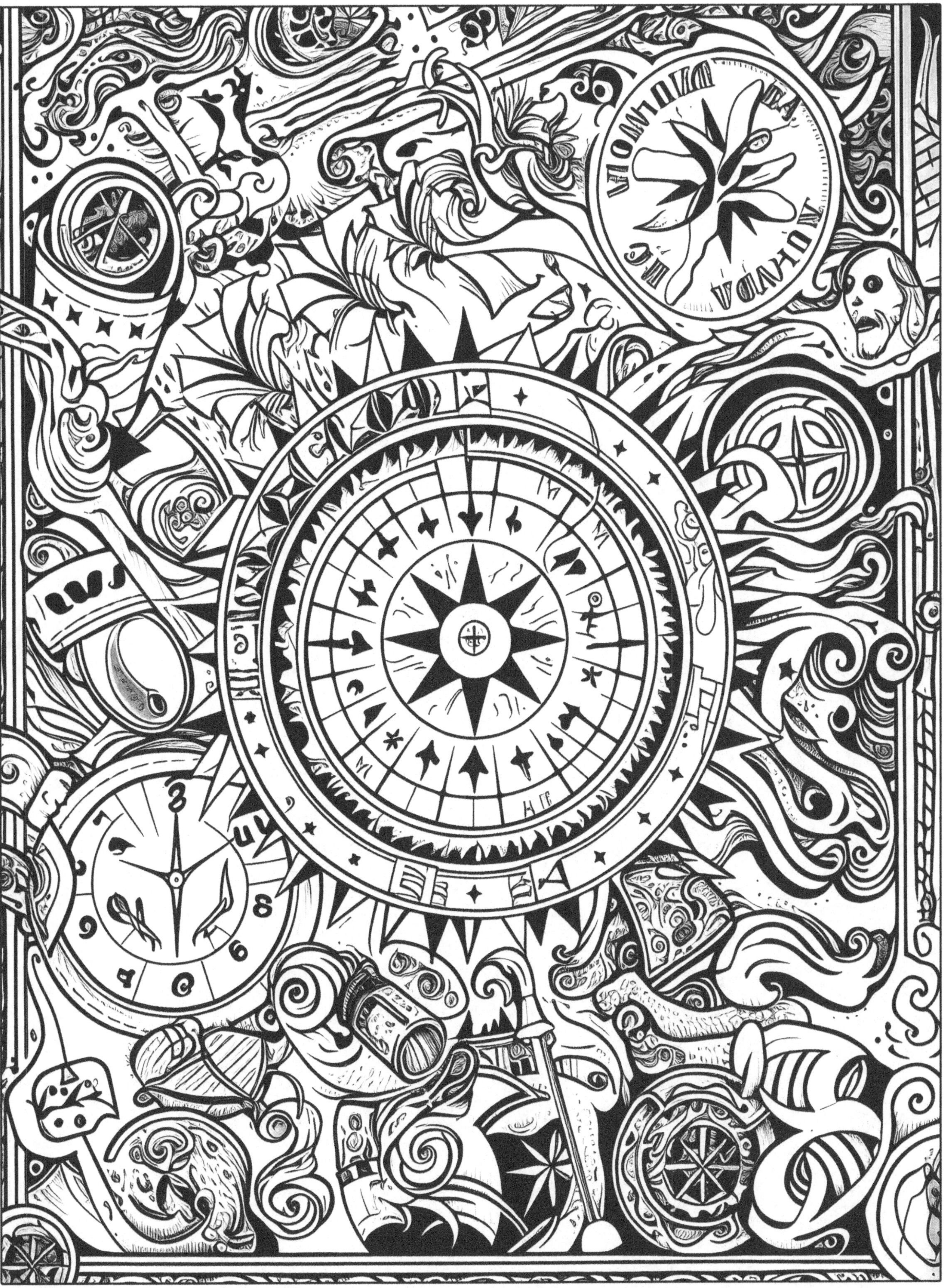

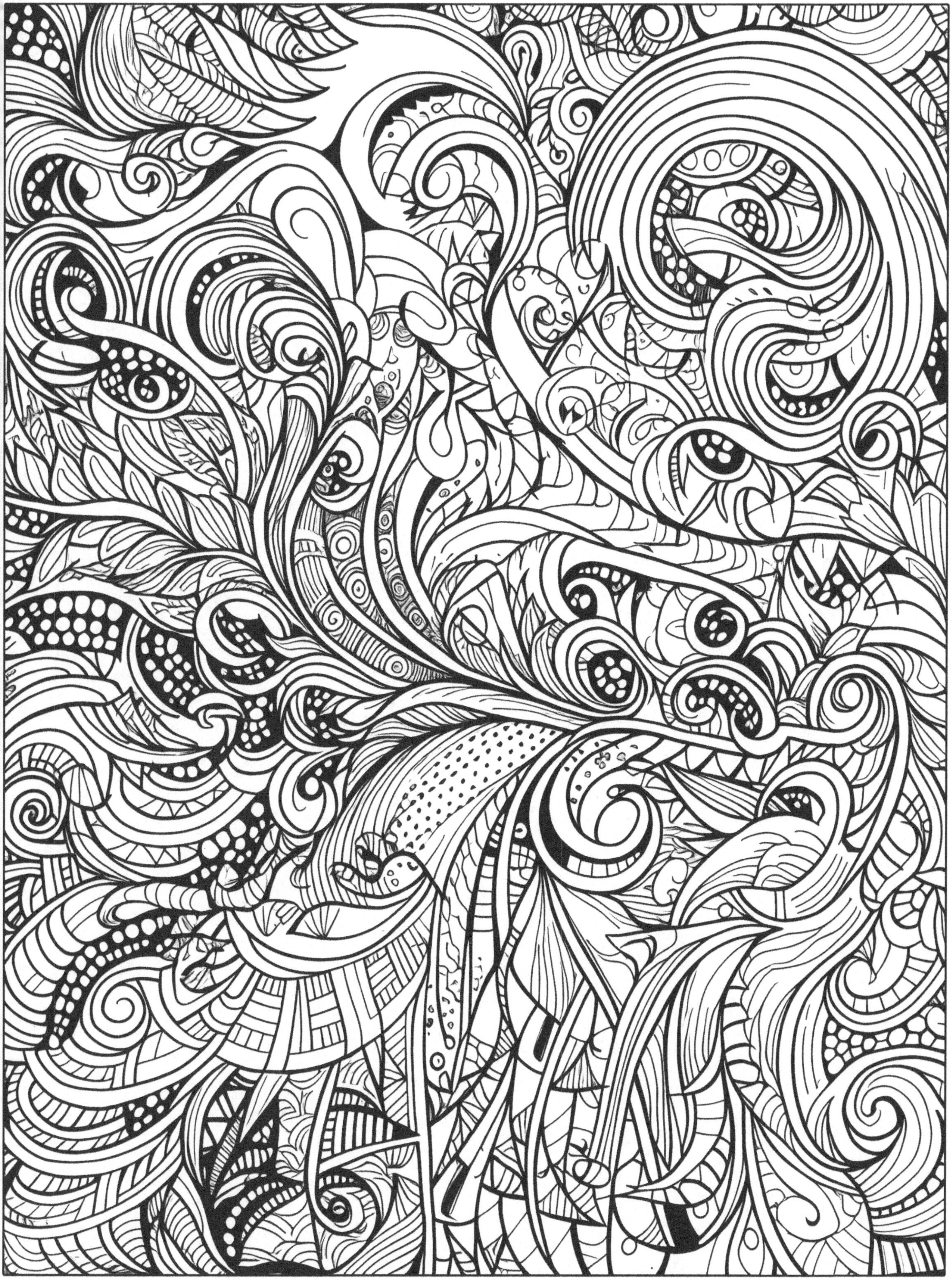

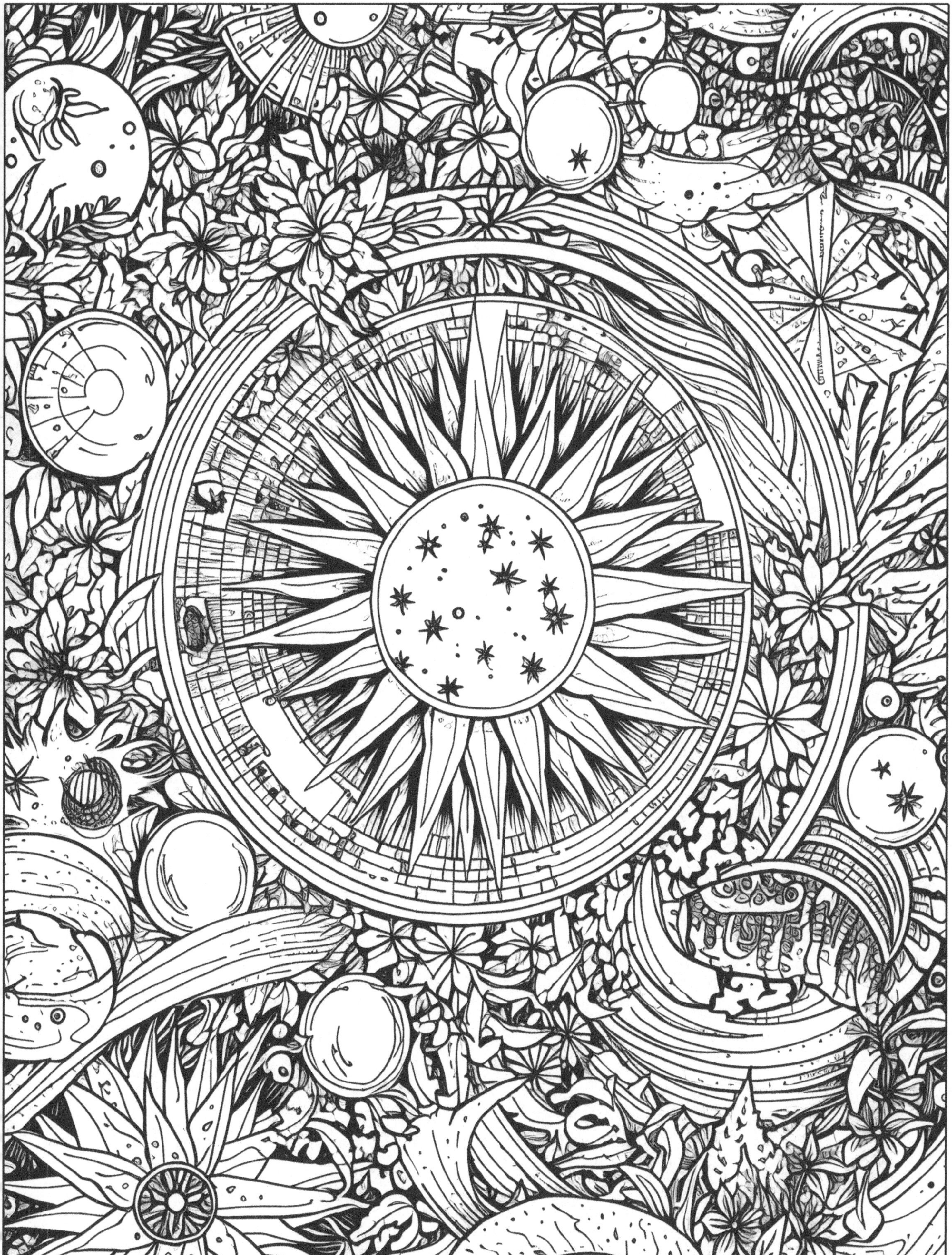

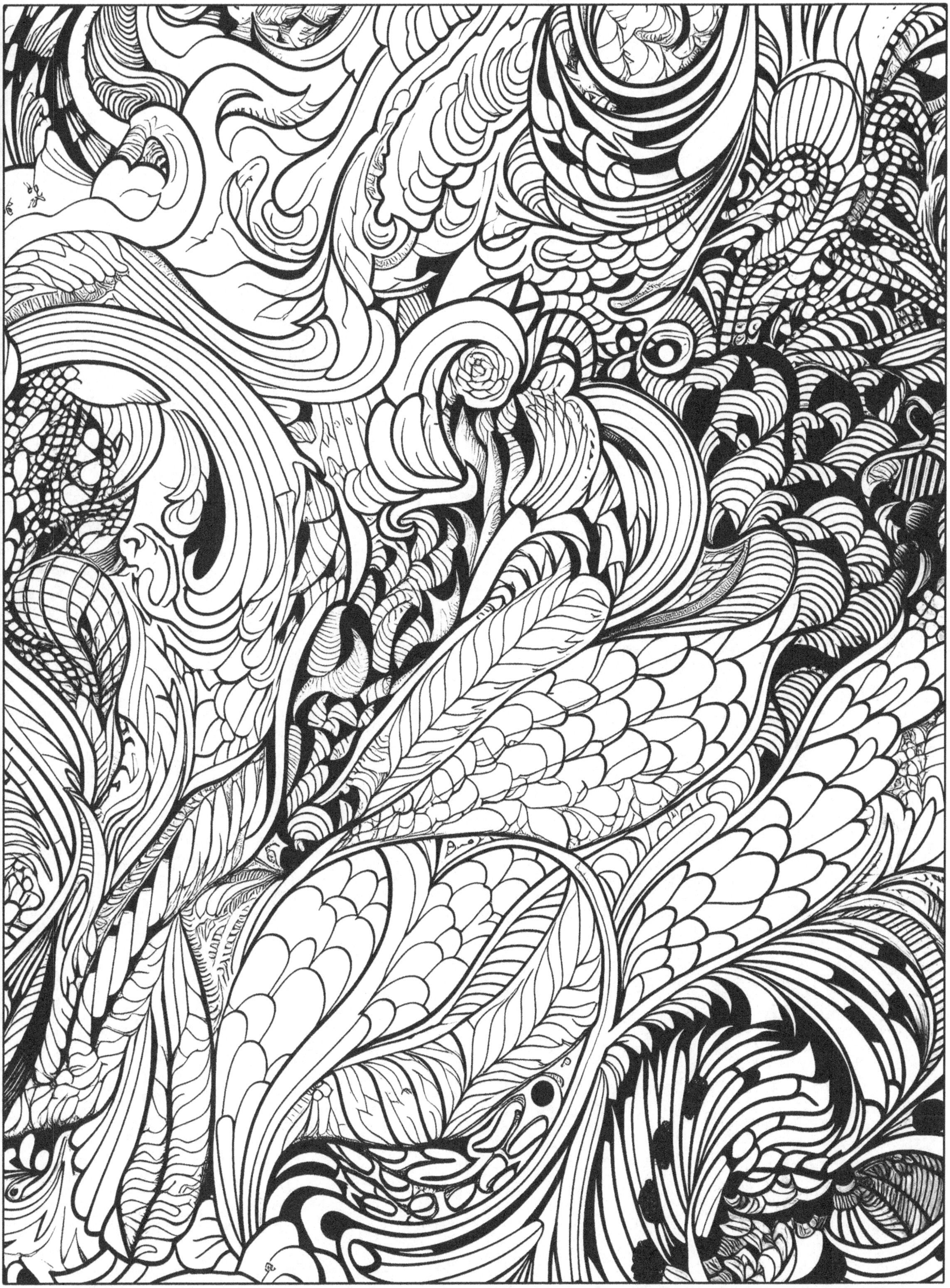

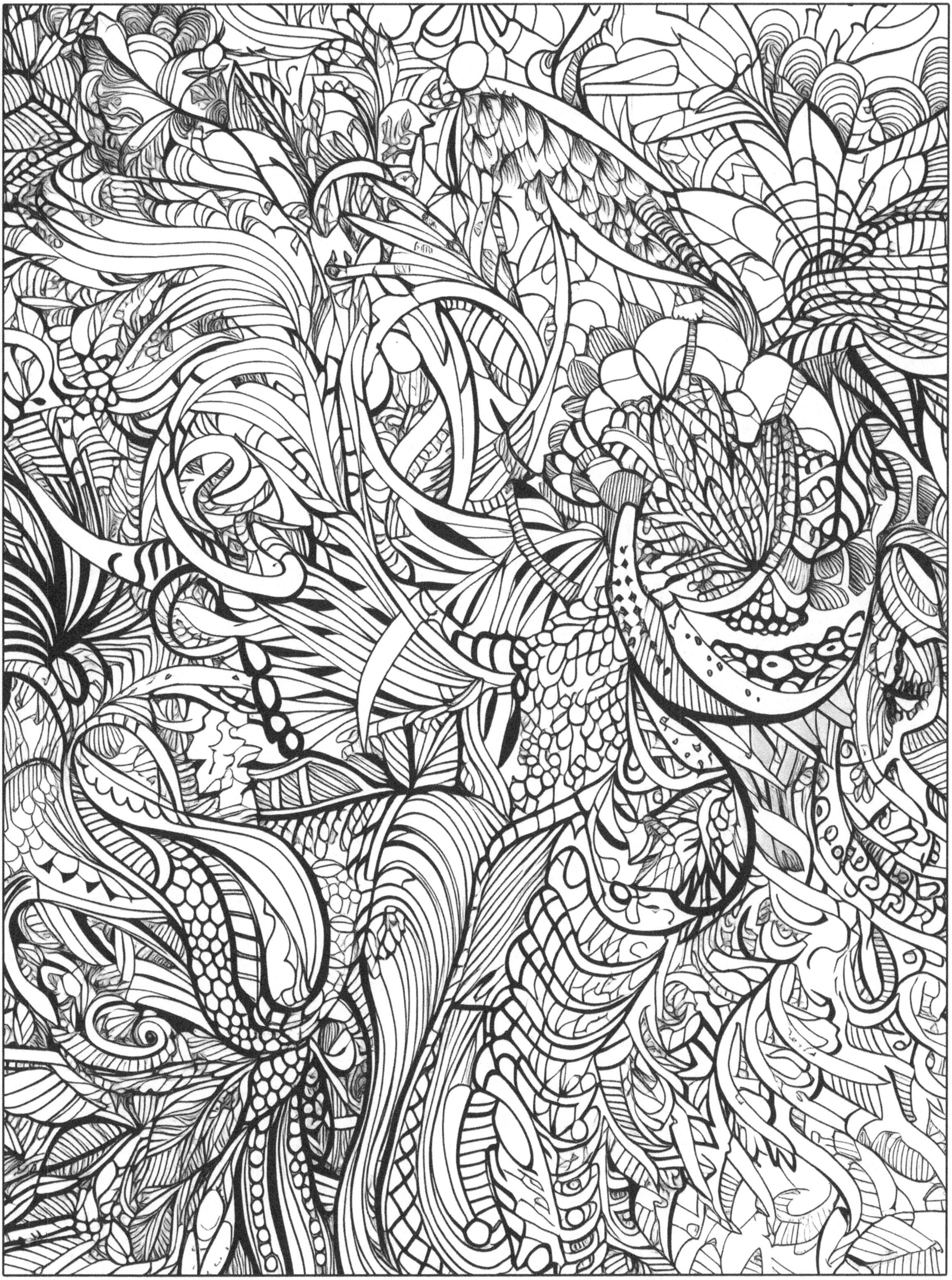

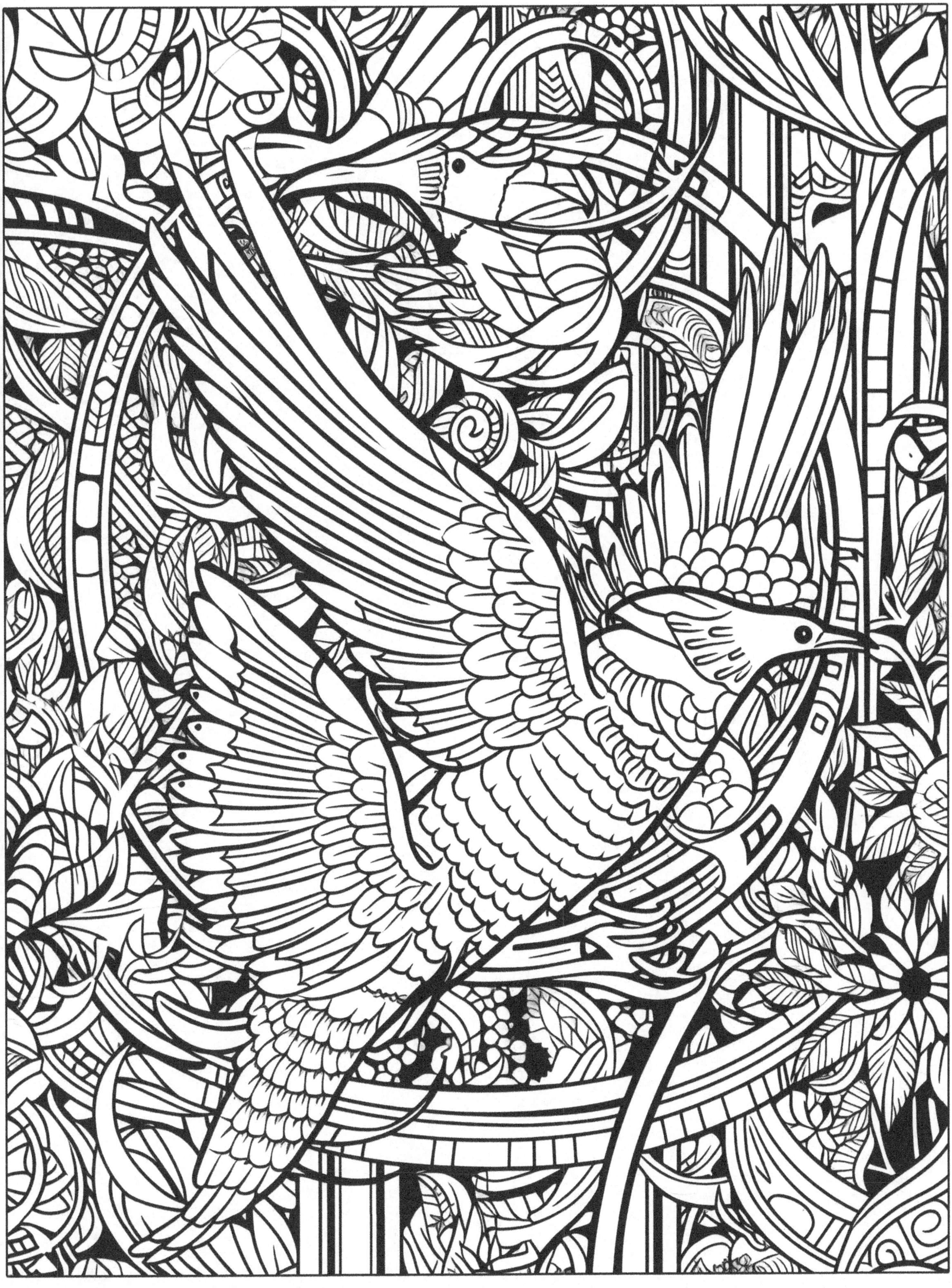

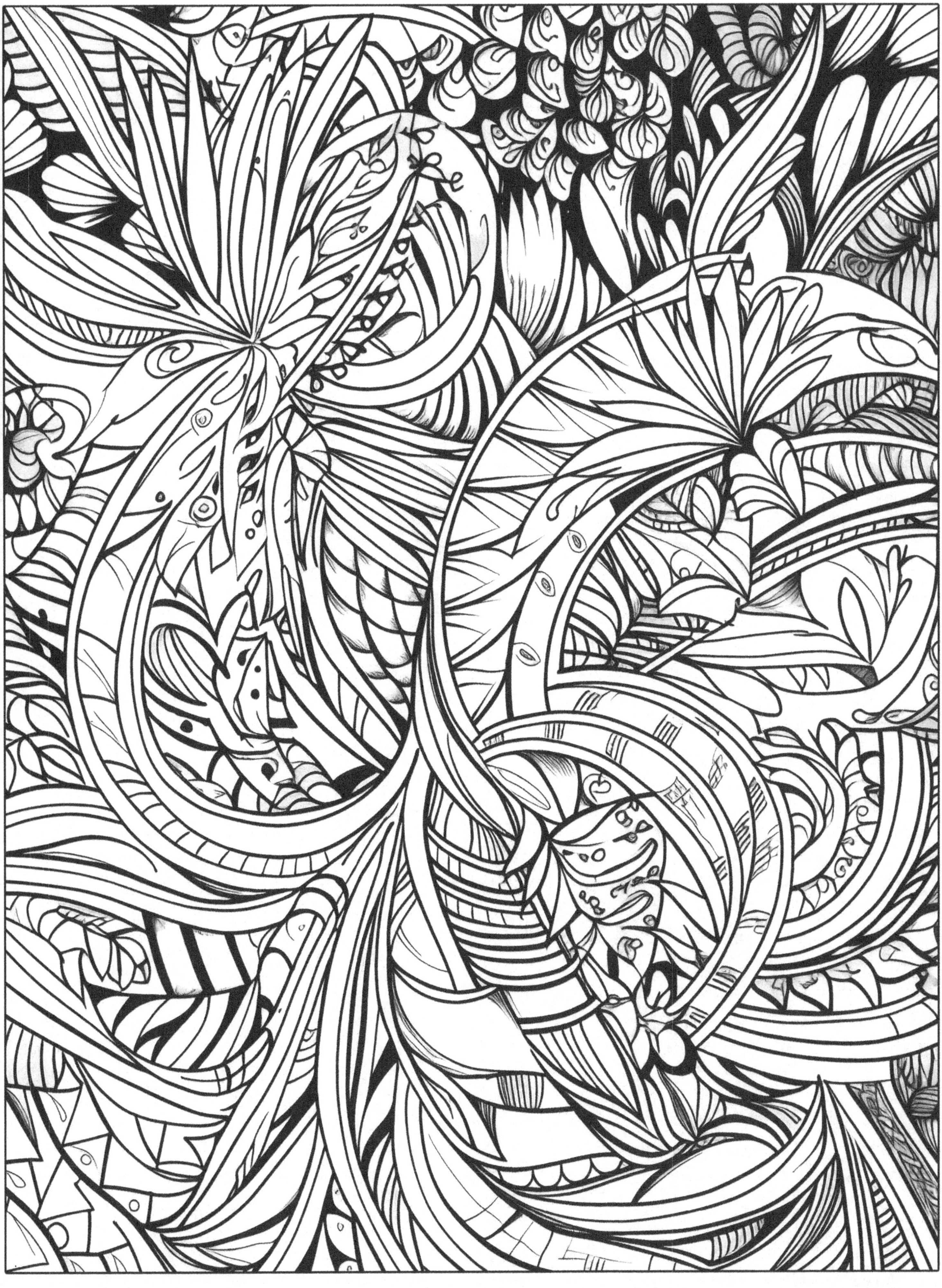

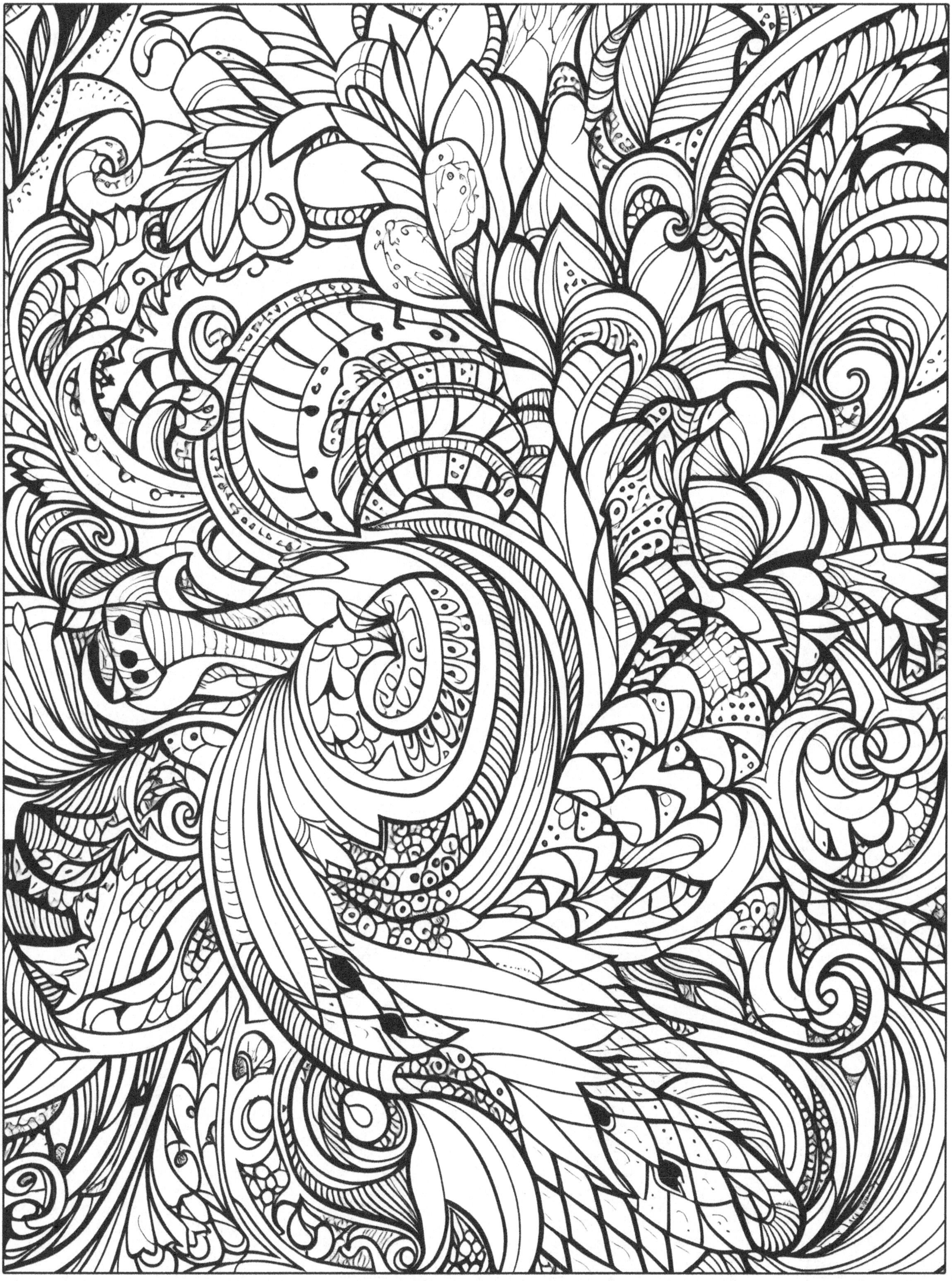

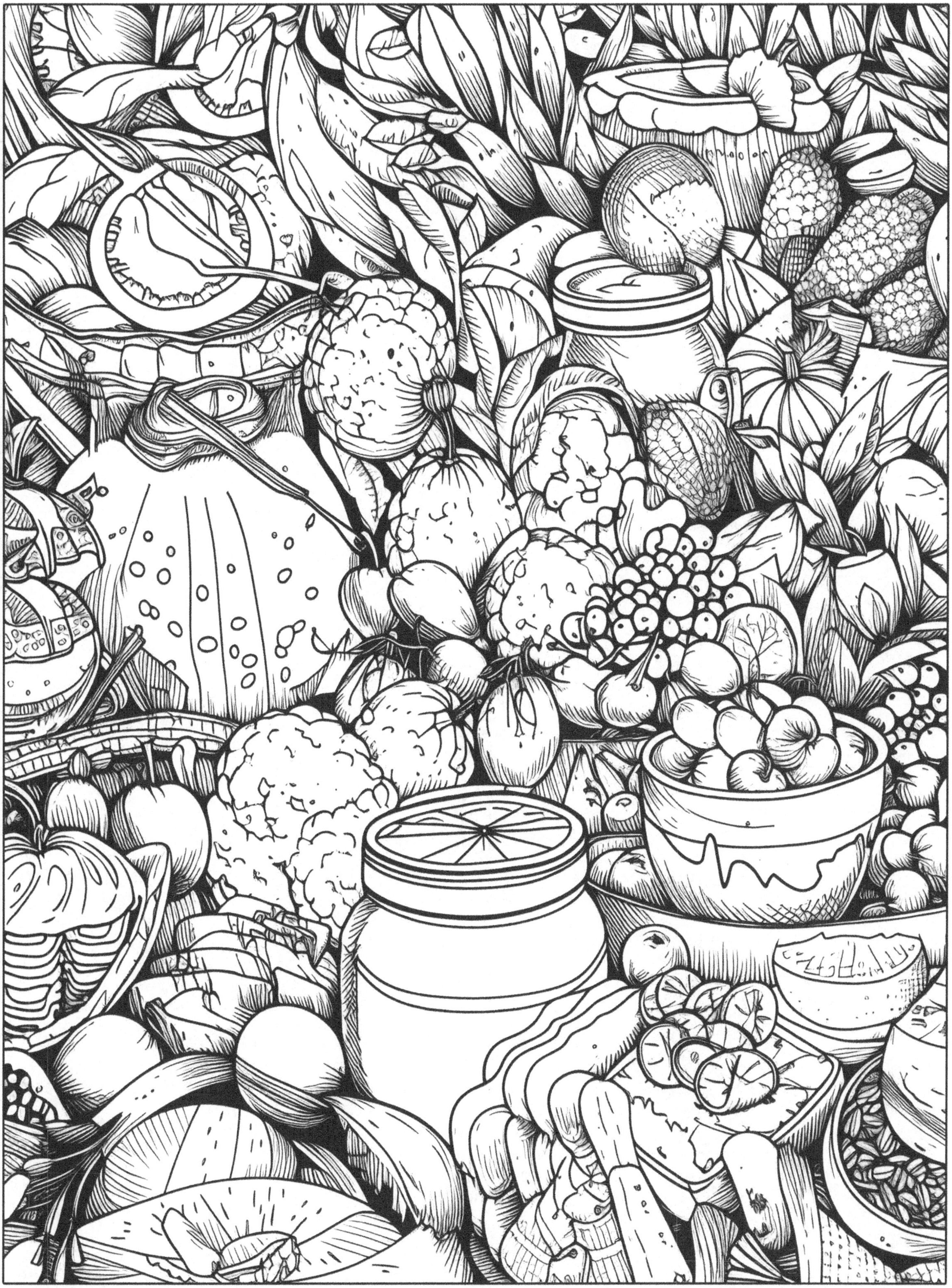

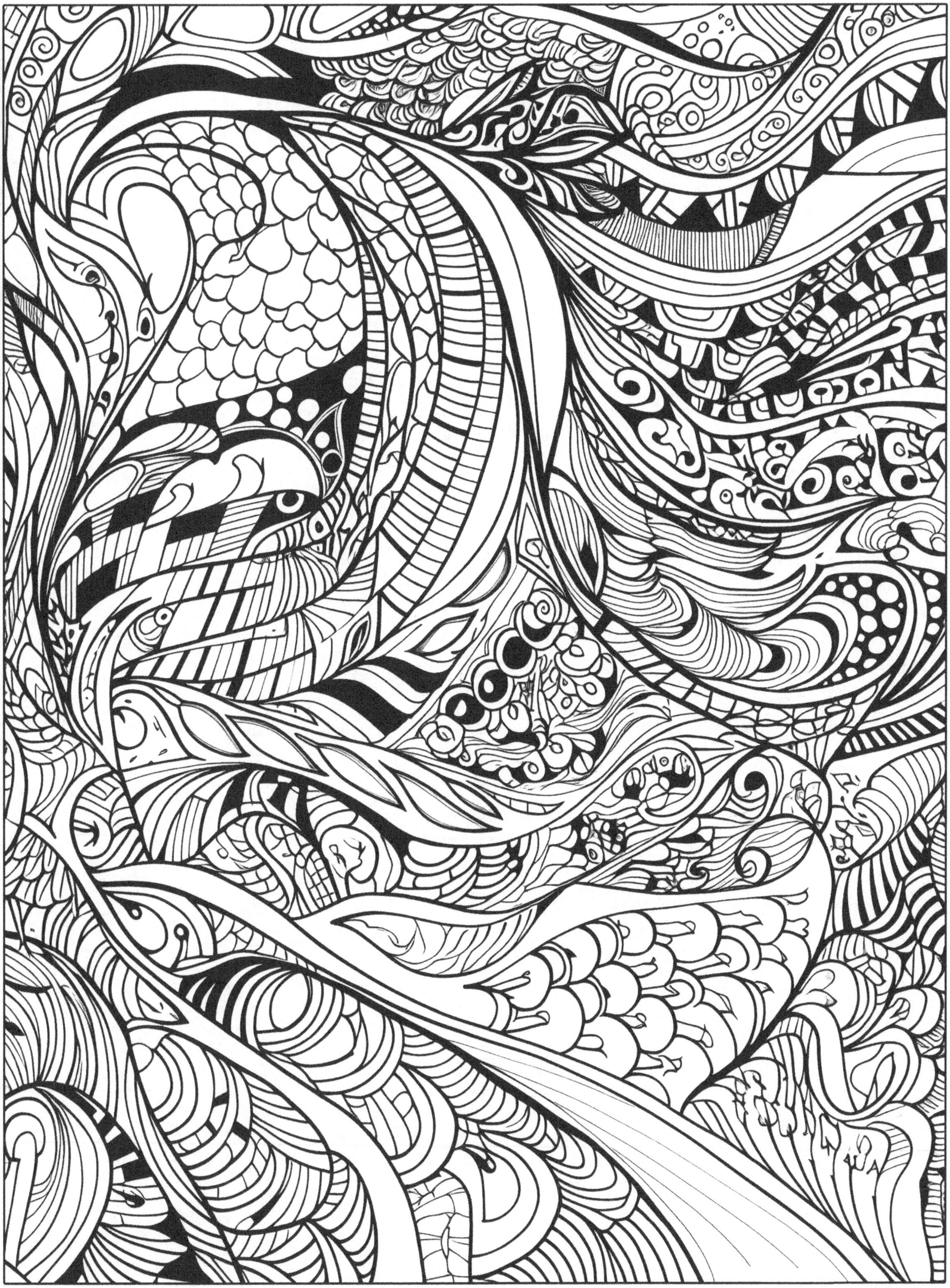

Made in United States
Orlando, FL
19 May 2023

33285450R00115